The Conjurer's Guide to

# St. Expedite

Denise M. Alvarado

The Conjurer's Guide to St. Expedite is published by Creole Moon Publications, Prescott Valley, AZ. 86312, USA. Copyright © 2014 Denise Alvarado. All rights reserved. Photographs and illustrations Copyright 2014, Denise Alvarado or are in the public domain.

ISBN-13: 978-1494301521 (paper)
ISBN-10: 1494301520 (paper)

Primary Category: Reference / Personal & Practical Guides
Country of Publication: United States
Publication Date: 12th Moon in the year 2014
Language: English

# CREOLE MOON

*Publications*

www.creolemoonpublications.com

# CONTENTS

*This book is devoted to the Minute Saint who has helped me beyond measure. Glory be to Saint Espidee!*

# FORWORD

Welcome to a world of word play, puns, mystery and legends, from the year 303 to the present, from Italy to France, Argentina, Brazil, Chile, the Philippines and finally, New Orleans, Louisiana. Welcome to the cult of devotion for the Minute Saint, whose past obscurity is replaced in special circles with near celebrity. Welcome to the world of St. Expedite. He's on the fringe of Catholicism, the "black sheep" of the saintly family; though, not through any fault of his own. Even as he is accused of being a novelty, a joke, and a mistake, even as he has suffered decanonization by the pope and decapitation by tempestuous followers, St. Expedite continues to work his miracles with expediency unlike any other saint. He is loyal to his devotees and they are loyal to him. He dispenses faith, hope and charity along with prosperity, work and justice all in one tight little bundle, wherever and however you need it. And, he will help near about anyone. Catholics, nonCatholics, pagans, rootworkers, Haitian Vodouisants and New Orleans Voudouists—really, anyone who petitions him with a sincere heart and the promise of a piece of pound cake (Sara Lee, preferably), he will come to their aid. Just be sure to let the world know how great he is when he comes through for you—that's about the only caveat.

When I first set out to write this book, I had no idea it would be as long as it is. One hundred and forty pages or so may not seem like a lot; but, for a saint who is best known for how little is known about him, it shows what a little digging can do. This book does not end my quest for learning all there is to know about this saint, however. That said, this book is the first and only book about St. Expedite that combines all the common knowledge with the uncommon knowledge, along with some of the mysteries of his presence in New Orleans Voudou, his relationship to Mardi Gras, Baron Samedi, and sorcery. I include an examination of entries about him in the Hyatt texts, as well as practical conjures of my own. All of the prayers you will ever need are contained within these pages—some of them are common Catholic prayers while others are prayers I have written using familiar Catholic format and verbiage. In short, this book contains everything a person needs to know about St. Expedite and how to serve him as a patron saint by anyone who cares to do so.

I looked high and low to find information on St. Expedite for this book. My thought is that everyone has a history, we just need to look until we find it. The task proved to be greater than I realized because there truly isn't a lot written about him, at least not in English. The French sure love this guy, however. Don't dare attempt to tell them he is some sort of hoax. Because when the French endear themselves to someone as much as they do St. Expedite, trying to relegate him to status of urban legend in the presence of a die hard French devotee will leave you feeling like *un parfait imbécile* (a complete idiot)!

But, it's not just the French who love St. Expedite. He is loved around the world and New Orleans is no exception. He is considered the patron saint of New Orleans by many, and the patron saint of New Orleans Voudou by many more. Where he is shunned by Roman Catholics, he is embraced by New Orleans Voudouists. He has a healthy following of those who appreciate folk Catholicism and a growing following of rootworkers. Despite being kicked off of the official martyrologies, downplayed on the Our Lady of Guadalupe Chapel website, ignored by devout Catholics and made fun of by Catholic priests, his cult of devotion remains strong. Try as they might, this saint's not going anywhere—fast

So, grab yourself a cup of coffee and chicory, or a glass of sweet tea if you prefer, put on something comfy and enjoy this labor of love I have created in perpetual homage to the Minute Saint. Glory be to St. Espidee!

Denise M. Alvarado,
December 2014

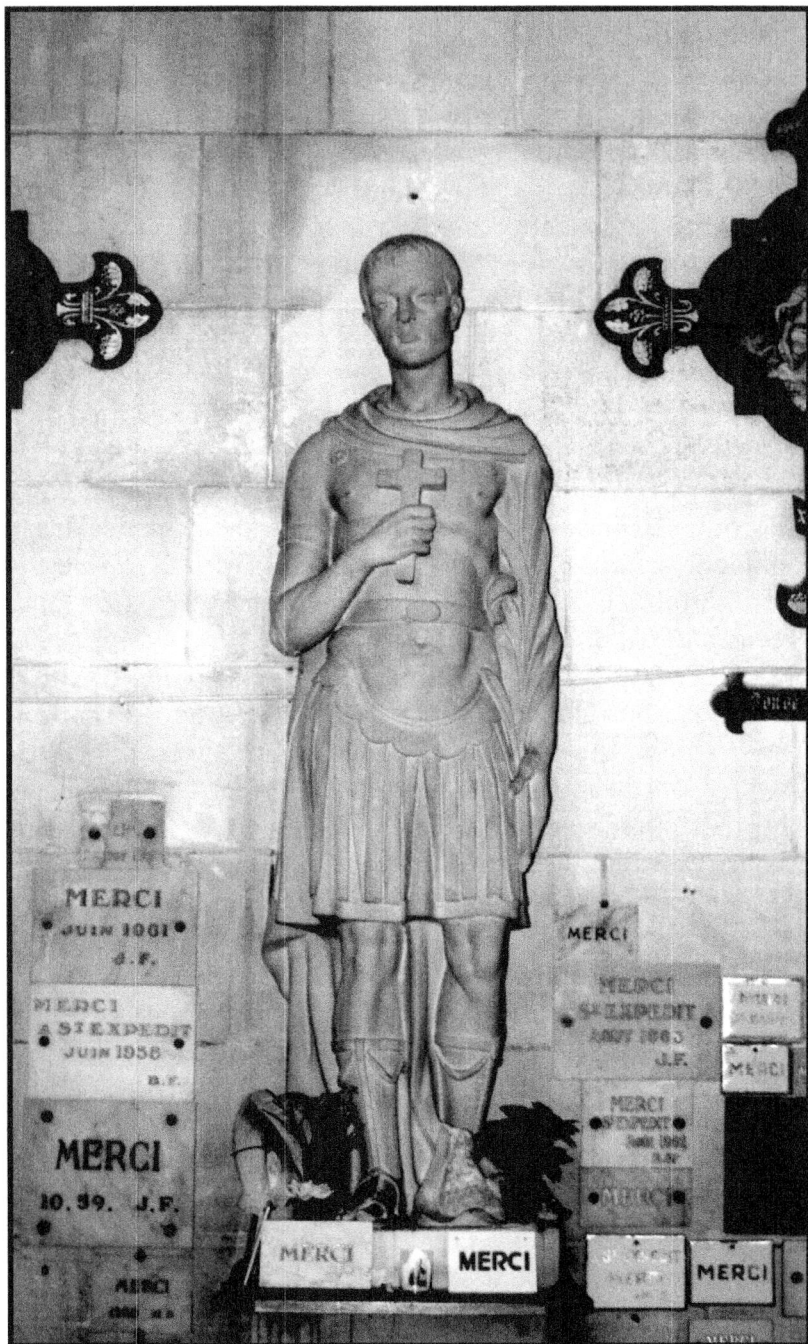

St Expedit in the Church of Pontaillac, Our Lady of the Angels Chapel, France. Photo © 2013 Llann Wé², Creative Commons Attribution-Share Alike 3.0 Unported license, Wikimedia Commons.

# CHAPTER ONE:
# INTRODUCTION

### Background and Origins, St. Expedite Around the World, St. Expedite and New Orleans Voudou, The Denial, In the News

H e could quite possibly be the most effective unofficial saint of urban legend ever to have been discovered. For a variety of reasons, the Roman Catholic Church will not officially recognize St. Expedite; but, at the same time, they won't discount him either. That's because he's just too damned popular. And, according to his devotees, he's just that damned good.

But that's okay, New Orleans Voudou has no problem embracing St. Expedite as one of her patron saints. And hoodoos, rootworkers, conjure doctors, spiritualists and sorcerers appreciate his worth, as well. No officialities are needed in these camps. Because when a saint works as well—and more importantly, as quickly—as St. Expedite works, he is more than welcome in the wide world of conjure.

In studying Louisiana religious cultures, St. Expedite rises to the forefront as a significant icon of the syncretic relationship between folk Catholicism and Creole Voudou. His unofficial status and questionable origin provides just the right amount of mystique to place him squarely on the shrines and in the hearts of anyone in need of a quick favor. Even in the Italian rural community of Independence, Louisiana, St. Expedito is publicly celebrated with feasting and festivities (Williams, 2011). And, in other parts of the world such as the French Island of Réunion, Argentina, Chile, the Philippines and Haiti, for example, St. Expedite can be found in varying degrees among diverse religiomagical landscapes.

Yet, popular as he may be in the pocket niches where he is found, he has spent most of his postmortem life in relative obscurity. Although he is very popular in New Orleans, the Catholic Church only tolerates him. Some people refuse to speak of him and others downright deny his very existence. For example, he is barely mentioned on the website for the Our Lady of Guadalupe chapel where his statue is housed. The denial and downplay does not diminish his influence among supplicants, though. In fact, it lends itself to his mystical appeal.

The use of wordplay and puns associated with St. Expedite's name is found in virtually all discussions about him. Referred to by informants in Harry Middleton Hyatt's *Hoodoo-Rootwork-Witchcraft-Conjuration* as the *Minute Saint*, St. Expedite is known by many other names as well, including *Expedite, Expedit, Expeditus, Expedito, Spedito, Espidee,* and *Spedee.* Never has there been a saint whose name describes so obviously and perfectly his patronage. Those invoking his intercession seek instant gratification and according to his devotees, that is the saint's main attraction.

But, who exactly is this saint of rapidity? According to legend, *Saint Expeditus* was a Roman Centurion in Armenia who decided to convert to Christianity. Before he did so, it is said the Devil appeared to him as either a crow or a snake and told him to put off following through with his decision until the next day (hence, his association with procrastination). Instead, Expeditus stomped on the animal and killed it, proclaiming, "I'll be a Christian today!" Unfortunately, St Expeditus met with the same fate as many Christian converts preceding him and was one of several other Armenian Christians—Saints Hermogenes, Gaius, Aristonicus, Rufus and Galata—beheaded during the Diocletian Persecution in Melitene (modern day Malatya, Turkey) on April 19th, 303. As a result, he became known as *Sant-Espedito di Melitene,* or *Saint Expedite of Melitene.*

The legend of St. Expedite is reflected in his iconography and associated puns. The Latin word, "expeditus," refers to a category of Roman foot soldier marching with a light load; thus, he is dressed as a Roman soldier (O'Brien, 2004). In one hand he holds the Christian symbol for martyrdom, the palm frond. His other arm stretches above his head and in his hand is held a cross inscribed with the word "Hodie," which is Latin for "Today." He stomps on a crow or raven with a ribbon in its beak, upon which is written the word "Cras," meaning "Tomorrow" in Latin. The crow is considered in the folklore of many cultures to be harbingers of death; this, and his placement in a mortuary chapel cements St. Expedite's association with death and dying—aspects of his character with which two-headed conjure doctors and sorcerer's strongly identify. In Germany, St. Expedite's imagery is slightly different; however, it portrays the same message—don't put off until tomorrow that which can be done today— as he is shown pointing at a clock.

Indeed, St. Expedite is the go-to saint for fast solutions to problems of all kinds. His quick response makes him extremely popular among those who strive to put an end to procrastination and delays and to those who seek financial success. He is petitioned for prompt solutions to business problems and has recently been coined the *Patron Saint of Nerds* due to his association with computer programmers and hackers. St. Expedite is also known as one of the lawyers of impossible causes, and as such, is petitioned for court cases and legal issues, as well. In France, his patronage focuses on youth and examinees as well as conflict resolution in relationships.

For as much as he is loved, most of St. Expedite's life is a mystery. Very little has been documented apart from the aforementioned legend describing him as a Roman Centurion; though, a plethora of origin stories exist surrounding the discovery of his statue—all variations on a familiar theme. The earliest reference to him, however, is in the fifth century **Martyrologium Hieronymianum** (meaning *Martyrology of Jerome*), which consists of lists of names of those individuals considered to be saints and martyrs, arranged according to the calendar order of feast days and anniversaries. He is listed in the *Martyrologium Hieronymianum* twice under the name "Expediti." The first listing is dated April 18:

"Romae Eleutheri episcopi et Anthiae matris eius et nii, ceri, Fabii, Proculi, Apollonii, Fortunati, Crispini, Parthenii, Caloceri, Fabii, Proculi, Apollonii, Fortunati, Crispini, **Expediti**, Mappalici, Victorini, Gagi."

The second listing is dated April 19:

"In Arminia Militana civitate Hermogeni, Gagi, **Expediti**, Aristonici, Rufi, Galatae una die coronatorum."

The general consensus seems to be that the April 18 listing was a mistake given he is known to have been beheaded for his beliefs on April 19. It is customary for saints' feast days to coincide with the dates of their deaths, so it is logical to assume April 19th is the correct feast day for St. Expedite. Apparently, such mistakes are not uncommon in the martyrologies. Because there are reportedly so many of these kinds of mistakes in them, some folks have opted to doubt St. Expedite's existence at all, chalking both entries up to a couple of typos and his existence as merely imaginary. This bizarre assertion, coupled with the fact that no official relics exist for St. Expedite, fueled Church skepticism in the early twentieth century and the Second Vatican Council (1962-1965) made the decision to remove St. Expedite (as well as St Christopher and St Philomena for other reasons), from the universal liturgical calendar.

Nonetheless, there is some historical evidence of the life and veneration of St. Expedite long before his arrival in New Orleans. In addition to his appearance in the 5th century Martyrology of Saint Jerome, his cult was also popular in Germany in the 18th century. Some have even suggested that veneration may have started back in the Middle Ages in Turin; although, I have only found reference to the Order of

Saints Maurice and Lazarus, a church dedicated to St John the Baptist, and numerous other martyrs (Benigni, 1913). Any reference to St. Expedite or any form of his name in medieval or present day Turin could not be located at the time of this writing.

In *The Legends of the Saints: An Introduction to Hagiography*, Delehaye (1907) discusses how the editor of the life of a saint must create a saint's profile based on the materials at their disposal. Often it is the place and method of martyrdom that is available and nothing more. When this is the case, the practice of associating the sound of the name of the saint with their alleged patronage is used. "Endowed with more or less imagination and fluency, innumerable hagiographers have resigned themselves to the necessity of supplementing the scarcity of documents by narratives founded on probability" (Delahaye, 1907, p. 92). He goes on to explain:

> The influence of sound on the popular impressions formed of certain saints is well known, and we are all aware that at times something little better than a pun decides the choice of a patron. Thus, in France, St Clare is invoked by those who suffer from their eyes because she enables people to see clearly; St Ouen cures deafness because he enables them to hear (ouïr); St Cloud cures boils (clous). Again, in certain parts of Germany St Augustine is believed to rid people of diseases of the eye (Auge) and in others of a cough (Husten). Writers have drawn up lists of these conceits, which are not solely due to popular imagination, and which learned men have amused themselves by multiplying. There is one of comparatively recent date which enjoys a surprising and regrettable popularity: St Expeditus, thanks to his name, has been acclaimed as the advocate of urgent causes. (Delehaye, 1907, p. 48).

In the footnotes, Delehaye makes an interesting reference: "St Expeditus, whose name is inscribed on the Hieronymian martyrology for the 18th or 19th of April under the rubric Melitincz in Armenia, has become in accordance with this method 'the valiant leader of the Thundering Legion' (See Dom Berengier, *Saint Expedit martyr en Armenie et patron des causes tirgentes in Missions catholiques, vol. xxviii.,* 1896, pp. 128-31. See also *Analecta Bollandiana, vol. xviii.,* p. 425 ; vol. xxv., pp. 90-98)." I mention this literary reference since it is one of a very few that mentions St Expeditus by name. And, the reference to him as the valiant leader of the *Thundering Legion* piqued my curiosity.

The *Thundering Legion* refers to the *Roman Theban Legion*, a Christian legion of soldiers during the reign of Diocletian. According to Ravenscroft (1987), a legion of 6,666 (or 6,600) Christian soldiers were called the Theban Legion because there were all enlisted from Thebias in Upper Egypt. The area around Thebes had a reputation for its zealous Christianity. The leaders of this legion were "Captain (Commanding Officer) Maurice, with his lieutenants Candid, the first commanding officer, and "Exuperius" the "Compidoctor"... Maurice, calling attention to the example of their faithful fellow soldiers, already martyrs, persuaded them all to be ready to die in their turn for the sake of their baptismal vow (the promise one makes at his baptismal to renounce Satan and his abominable service and to worship only God)" (Ravenscroft, 1987). While the context of this account is consistent with the accounts of St. Expedite's murder by beheading occurring during the Diocletian persecution in 303, none of the names of those in the legion from this source can be found when cross-referenced with those listed in the *Martyrology of Jerome* on either the 18th or 19th of April. That said, the list of names is incomplete and so a thorough cross-referencing of the names is impossible to accomplish based on these two unreliable sources.

On the other hand, there is an account of a Thunder Legion in reference to Melitene on the French website *Hodie.* According to this account, St. Expedite was the commander of the XII Roman Thundering Legion, who held its neighborhoods in the city of Melitene, capital of the Roman province of Armenia. He had 6821 Armenian Christian soldiers under his command. The name *Thundering Legion* came from an act of miraculous weapons. It was during the reign and in the presence of Marcus Aurelius himself when the Roman army, engaged in the arduous campaign of Germany, had become entrenched in a fortified settlement of Quades in northeastern Hungary. Surprised by the barbarians (Germans), the Romans had left circle. It was summer and there was a drought. Dying of thirst, the Roman soldiers no longer had the strength to fight; their morale was declining rapidly. The Roman army was about to be destroyed entirely.

Appealing to the magical omens that inevitably accompanied the troops in the field, and which predicted the good or bad end of a campaign, Marcus Aurelius ordered public prayers and offerings to the gods. While the rest of the army engaged in pagan invocations and practices, the Thundering Legion left the camp, knelt on the fields and prayed fervently to their Christian God. Seeing over 6000 soldiers kneeling, arms outstretched, the enemy took advantage and attacked.

At the same time their prayers were completed, the soldiers engaged the Germans. At that moment, a torrential rainstorm complete with thunder, lightning and hail began to fall. The soldiers collected in their helmets this water of Divine Providence and drank to regain their strength. Lightning riddled the ranks of the barbarians who fled under a rain of hail as big as stones while Christians were unaffected. It is in commemoration of this miracle that Marcus Aurelius gave the XII Roman Legion the name *Thundering Legion*.

Apparently there are separate accounts of this miracle, corroborated by Apollonius, Saint Euseius and Tertellian. In Rome, the miraculous event of the Thundering Legion is captured in stone relief on the Antonine Column, which depicts God making it rain and the hail which decimated the Germans.

# St. Expedite's Origin Story in France

O nce upon a time, in approximately 1781, Paris, France, a crate containing the body of a saint from the Denfert-Rochereau catacombs in Paris was delivered to a community of nuns there. The catacombs, known as "The World's Largest Grave," are underground ossuaries that hold the remains of approximately 6 million people. The catacombs were created at the end of the 18th century and are contained in a renovated section of caverns and tunnels that are the remains of Paris' historical stone mines (Musée de France, n.d.).

The crate received by the nuns had the word **SPEDITO** written on it. In this story, the nuns make *un petit faux pas*, attributing **SPEDITO** for the name of the martyr. When they prayed to St. Expedite for his intercession, their prayers were answered so quickly that reports of his rapid response spread like wildfire throughout Catholic countries. Thus began the concerted effort to spread a cult of devotion to "the saint who could make things happen in a hurry."

While this is an interesting origin story, it is by no means the only one. There are reports of identical stories coming out of Sao Paulo, Brazil, Haiti and New Orleans. Moreover, the similarities between origin stories are quite remarkable.

Today, no chapel exists that is dedicated specifically to St. Expedite in Paris; however, a beautiful statue of St. Expedite is on display in the Chapel of Our Lady of Good Deliverance in Neuilly, Rue d' Argençon in Paris. Devotees also reportedly pray at the Church of St. Roch.

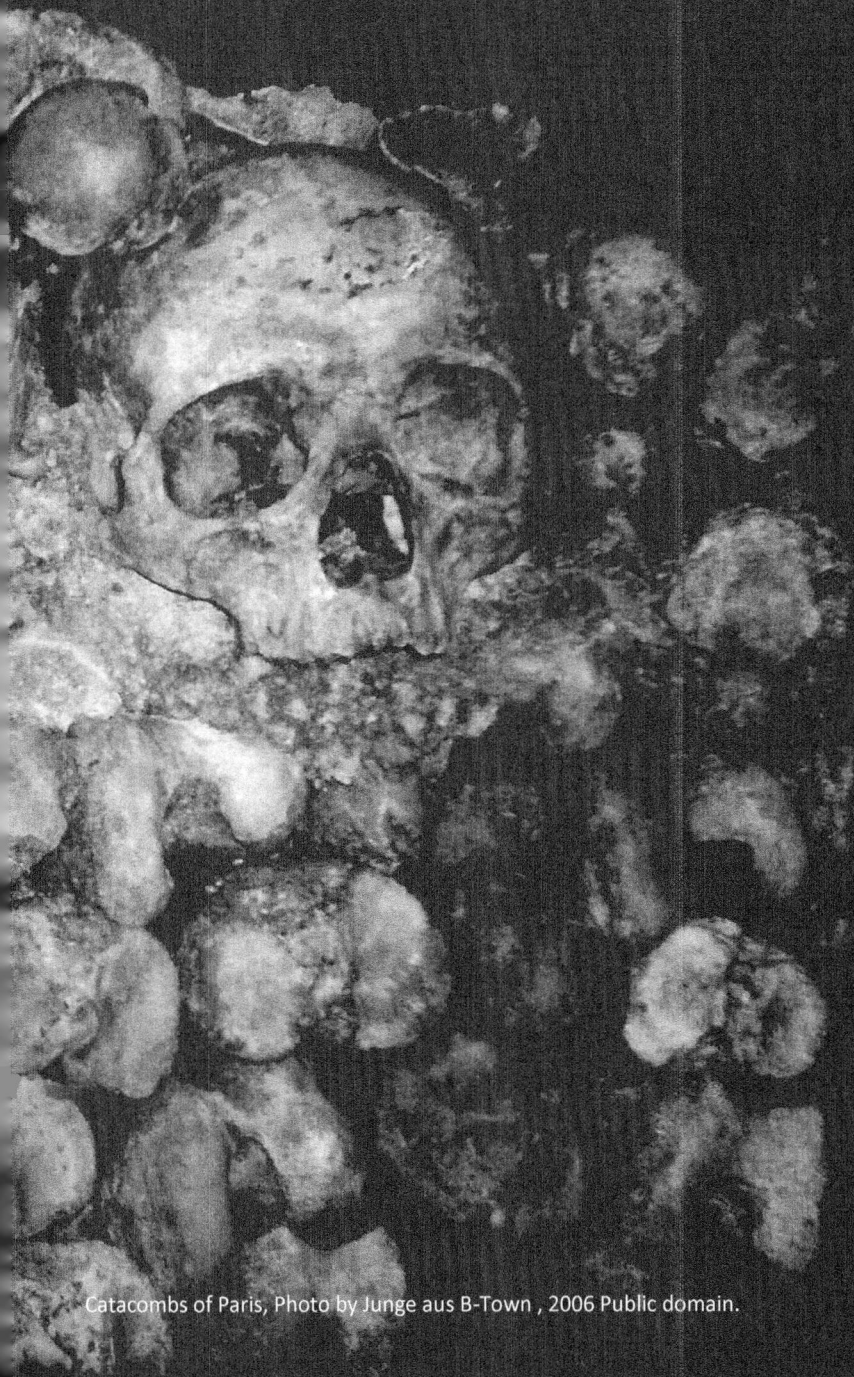

Catacombs of Paris, Photo by Junge aus B-Town , 2006 Public domain.

# St. Expedite around the World

## Road Side Altars in Réunion

Today, St. Expedite remains a popular folk saint in various parts of the world. He is extremely popular on the tiny French Island of Réunion, located off the east coast of Madagascar in the Indian Ocean. Reunion Island is a diverse community consisting of white Europeans, Indians, Africans, Chinese, and Vietnamese. The origin of his devotion here follows the familiar storyline of the arrival of a mysterious crate marked *expedit* that contained some bones. Apparently, a request was made by colonials to the Vatican for saintly relics. When the box of old bones arrived with *expedit* marked on the wooden box, those who received them assumed they were the bones of a saint and named him St. Expedite.

An additional dimension of his story indicates St. Expedite is routinely invoked for his help with black magic in placing and breaking curses. As the story goes, he is so prompt to dispense a curse that to call him anything other than St. Expedite would make no sense, whatsoever.

However he arrived here and whatever the nature of his association, people professing a wide range of religious faiths including Christianity, animism, Buddhism, and Hinduism are equally as attracted to his ability to get things done in a hurry, whether it be a curse or a blessing.

Apparently, St. Expedite is revered in secret in Reunion; some have gone so far as saying it is a taboo to invoke him. People typically do not come out during the day to make their petitions so as to avoid being seen. That said, there are roadside altars, huts, little shrines and niches all over painted in bright red that do nothing to keep St. Expedite on the downlow. Images of these roadside altars show they are obviously well taken care of and offerings or *ex votos* commonly left at the various shrines in gratitude for petitions granted show his devotees are numerous and strong in faith. Among the offerings left are red wine and small cakes with coins pressed into them.

Inside a roadside hut altar dedicated to Expeditus on Réunion Island CC BY-SA 3.0 Uploaded by David.Monniaux (2005) Wikimedia Commons.

Unlike other places, there is an unusual practice here that is not observed in other areas of St. Expedite devotion. Apparently, as easy as it is to observe how well cared for the road side altars are, it is also plain to see decapitated statues of St. Expedite strewn about—reportedly the result of petitioners' anger for when he doesn't come through for them. It has also been suggested that he is decapitated as part of a petition to break existing curses.

I find the practice of decapitating his statue to be quite intriguing. Conjecture found in one newspaper article I found about it says nothing more than I have shared thus far. Given the different cultural influences found in Réunion, it makes me wonder who may have brought the practice with them and what the true meaning is for cutting off St. Expedite's head.

Interestingly, there is the theme of decapitation found in private and royal funerary literature of ancient Egypt (Picardo, 2007). The actual act of decapitation was considered the most reprehensible of acts with only the most vile of human beings deserving of such a fate. To the ancient Egyptians, enemies and foreigners were among those who received such treatment at the request of the King. However, decapitation also occurred in a ritual context in magic spells. Symbolic decapitations directed against enemies and criminals were invoked through execration magic and in threat-formulae or curses against robbers. Evidence for this activity is found in some tomb inscriptions.

Of course, the possibility that St. Expedite is being destroyed by iconoclasts shouldn't be discounted. *Iconoclasm* is the deliberate destruction of religious icons or monuments, usually for religious or political motives. In common parlance, an iconoclast is a person who challenges cherished beliefs or traditional institutions as being based on error or superstition (Besançon & Todd, 2000). Could it be there are locals who disapprove of St. Expedite and show their disapproval by the destruction of his statues? Whatever the case may be, it is clear there is an underground devotion of St. Expedite that serves both positive and nefarious purposes on the island of Réunion.

## Devotion in Argentina

A serious devotional following of St. Expedite also exists in Argentina. There is a chapel called *San Expedito* located in the Province of San Juan, in a little town called Bermejo. Bermejo has only one hundred inhabitants and has no hotels, bars or restaurants. This town became known as the epicenter of the earthquake of 1977. The chapel is considered very humble, with white walls, tiles and wooden roof gable. The pews are covered with cushions of different kinds, colors and shapes. Thanks to the chapel of San Expedito, the obscure little town has grown and every year on his Feast Day, April 19th, the town is invaded by more than 20,000 people.

The image of the saint of fast results and urgent cases arrived in San Juan about 30 years ago, when some people coming from Buenos Aires went to Bermejo to help a woman named Doña Petronila Mercado de Lucero. As the story goes, St. Expedite helped Doña Petronila's husband overcome his addiction to alcohol, awakening a deep faith in St. Expedite among the locals. The house of Doña Petronila was the first chapel of St. Expedite. The Bermejo community continues to this day to worship the saint.

## Veneration in Chile

The Santa Maria de los Angeles Church in the Reñaca sector of Viña has a huge shrine for San Expedito, called the *Santurario de San Expedito*. It is a popular pilgrimage site, where they hold a special mass every month on the 19th for devotees of the saint. Hundreds of plaques are plastered on the walls of the shrine saying "thank you" for answered prayers. The saint of just and urgent causes first made his appearance in Chile when a devotee brought his image to the Viña del Mar beach. The woman was determined to have a shrine built for him there but the local authorities were against the idea. So, she asked some priests to pray a novena with her to San Expedito to make it happen. In less than nine days, they were granted approval to build the church. Since that time, devotion to San Expedito has grown to include people from all walks of life.

## Expéditions of Haitian Vodou

If you ask a Haitian Vodouisant about the role of St. Expedite in Haitian Vodou today, they will likely state St. Expedite is syncretized with Baron La Croix and Guede Limbo, both of whom are ancestral lwas or spirits. In Alfred Métraux's book

*Voodoo* in which he describes his observations of Haitian Vodou religious phenomenon during his time there as an anthropologist from 1948 to 1950, he makes mention of St. Expedite (spelled in the book Saint *Expedit*) as associated with a type of death conjure, and in particular, with *l'envoi morts* or *Expéditions*, meaning *Sending of the Dead*. While Voodoo is introduced in the book by Dennis Wheatley as "the most bestial, cruel and depraved of all religions," Métraux nonetheless provides one of the only ritual descriptions of St. Expedite working with Baron Samedi ever recorded. This makes it valuable to the present discussion.

According to Métraux, Expéditions are a type of death curse in which the dead are sent to harm someone. St. Expedite's image is turned upside down and he is invoked to rally the dead for nefarious purposes with the following prayer:

> *Almighty God, my Father, come and find so-and-so that he may be "disappeared" (sic) before me like the thunder and lightning. Saint Expedit, you who have the power to move the earth, you are a saint and I a sinner. I call on you and take you as my patron from today. I am sending you to find so-an-so, rid me of (expédiez) his head, rid me of his memory, rid me of his thought, rid me of his house, rid me of all my enemies, visible and invisible, bring down on them thunder and lightning. In thine honor Saint Expedit, three Paters."* (Métraux, (1959, p. 273).

The three Paters stated at the end indicates the petitioner should say three Our Fathers following this prayer (see page 136).

If the curse is successful, the victim will begin to show signs of spitting blood, growing thin and finally dying if not caught and treated in time by a qualified Houngan.

Still, whether or not the curse works depends on Baron Samedi who is the head loa of the Dead. The Baron is the one who makes the ultimate decision as to who lives and who dies. Thus, it is imperative that the bokor (sorcerer) invoking

St. Expedite also make an attempt to persuade the Baron that the curse is a good idea. Therefore, the bokor must strike the ground three times with his machete while calling out Baron Samedi's name and at midnight, he must make an offering of bananas and chopped potatoes at the foot of the cross in the cemetery that symbolizes him. Then, the bokor collects a handful of grave dirt from each of the Dead who he intends to send and spreads it in the path where the victim must walk—a practice referred to as "foot track magic" in New Orleans hoodoo. In addition to gathering the grave dirt for use in foot track magic, the bokor may also gather stones from any grave, knowing that within each stone resides a Dead soul who must work for the bokor when called upon. This is done by throwing a stone against the door of the victim; at the point of contact, the Dead soul is released upon the victim and revenge is insured (Métraux, 1959).

In addition to sending the dead to inflict harm on a per-

## THE GUÉDÉ

Guédé, meaning, "Guardian of the Dead," is one of the major family of ancestral spirits in both the Haitian Vodou and New Orleans Voudou religions. Baron Samedi is the head of the Guédé, and is considered one of the patron loas of New Orleans and St. Expedite, with whom he is syncretized, is considered a patron saint of New Orleans. Baron Samedi is the ultimate suave and sophisticated spirit of Death, typically depicted as if ready to be buried Haitian style with a top hat, black tuxedo, dark glasses, and cotton plugs in the nostrils. He has a white, mostly skull-like face and speaks with a nasal tone of voice, and tells crude but funny jokes. The first burial of a man in any cemetery in Haiti is dedicated to Baron Samedi. His wife is the lwa Manman Brigit.

son, the Dead may be sent to possess livestock. The Dead's presence causes the animal to go mad which forces the owner of the animal to slaughter it. Métraux indicates jealousy and vengeance are prime motivators for sending the Dead to possess livestock.

Another accounting of ritual work with St. Expedite is found in Ray Malbrough's (2003) *Hoodoo Mysteries*. In this book, he discusses the creation of an ancestor pot and likens St. Expedite to Baron LaCroix. Part of the ceremony for creating the pot involves the recitation of a number of prayers, including prayers to St Anthony, St Gerard and St. Expedite, followed by some standard Catholic prayers and the sign of the cross. The remaining invocation refers to the Haitian lwas, including Baron LaCroix, invoked by name.

Malbrough also refers to the practice of Expéditions in Louisiana and Haiti in *Hoodoo Mysteries*. In Malbrough's description, Expéditions are worked by buying the spirits of three dead people with the aid of St. Expedite (as Baron La-Croix). A black candle is left at the tomb of each spirit that is hired to do the working. In Louisiana Voodoo and hoodoo, a significant amount of conjure work is accomplished at the cemetery, and it is always customary to pay the spirits of the Dead for services rendered and for the removal of grave dirt from their grave sites. As in Métraux's description, some grave dirt from each of the graves is collected and tossed where the intended target will walk over it or otherwise come in contact with it.

Both Métraux and Malbrough describe a ritual to buy back a person's life when divination has revealed the individual has become the victim of *l' envoi morts*. The ritual is not for the squeamish as it involves burying a rooster or hen alive. I won't share the details of the ritual for this reason. However, the gist of the ritual is such that a deal is presented to Baron Samedi to reverse the death curse, as he is the only one who can do so, and St. Expedite is invoked to transfer the curse from the person into the rooster or hen. The rooster or hen is buried alive and a banana tree is planted over the rooster's grave. There are conflicting accounts as to what happens from this point forward. According to Métraux, if the banana tree lives, the person will die within one year. If the banana tree dies, it indicates Baron Samedi has accepted the deal and the individual's life will be spared. On the other hand, Malbrough indicates that if the banana tree lives, "the person's life is saved for the time being. If the banana tree dies, it is decided by the Guede that the person should die" (Malbrough, 2003, p. 153).

You may be wondering, why a banana tree? In Vodou, the banana tree represents the "first and greatest of the houn'gans (Adam), just as it is the tree of the first and most learned of mam'bos (Eve, whom voodooists call Erzulie). Now, the Tree of Adam is identified in the traditional magic, with the fig tree of the scriptures. " (Rigaud, 1953, pp. 98-99). It's fruit, the banana is therefore, the fruit of knowledge. The banana tree "never ceases to renew itself by its shoots. It's perpetual outgrowings symbolize eternal life" (Rigaud, p. 99).

## St. Expedite in Independence, Louisiana

Moving away from Haitian Vodou, we turn our attention to the largely Sicilian and Italian community of Independence, Louisiana. Here, we find St. Expedite by the name of *St. Expedito*. He became popular in the community when a chapel was built in the late 1940s in his honor after he helped someone in a very big way. According to Karen Williams (2011):

In the '50s and '60s the pavilion was packed with people eating and drinking. Differing from New Orleans' custom of feeding the saint, the Italians made sure to feast with him, not limiting the food to one simple cake to leave for the saint's benefit, but feasting on hotdogs garnished with a local specialty, Hi Ho barbeque sauce, made in the community, along with soft drinks and beer, while the festivities included dancing and music by local bands like the Rhythm Kings. (Williams, 2011, par. 8, lines 8-14).

The chapel in Independence is aptly called *St Expedito*, and is complete with a couple of portraits of the saint, plaster appendages representing body parts that had been healed (reminiscent of St. Roche in New Orleans) and, of course, a statue. There was actually a St. Expedito Society active there for 80 years. Celebrations used to be held every second Sunday in June in honor of the saint During the 1980s; although, membership in the society waned and so did the activities (Marciano 2005, as cited in Williams, 2011). The chapel itself apparently remains and is used periodically for special functions.

## St. Expedite in New Orleans

The origin of St. Expedite in New Orleans is related to the construction of the Our Lady of Guadalupe Chapel, International Shrine of St Jude (Old Mortuary Chapel). And, depending on who you talk to will determine which version of the story you receive. Built in 1826 as a funeral chapel for victims of yellow fever, Our Lady of Guadalupe Chapel was strategically constructed near St Louis Cemetery No. 1 so as to minimize the spread of disease throughout the Quarter. The unknown dead were moved through the mortuary's back door directly into the cemetery right across the street. According to one legend, in the early 1900s some priests sent off to Spain for a large statue of the Virgin Mary and months later, two crates arrived by ship. One crate contained the statue of Mary, which was expected. The other crate, however, had the word **ESPEDITO** stamped on the outside. When the priests opened the second crate, they found the statue of a saint depicted as a Roman Centurion. Apparently, the priests did not recognize the identity of the saint and mistook the stamp for the name of the saint. And so, the unidentified statue of the Roman Centurion has been known as St. Expedite ever since, or so the story goes.

But wait, there's more.

Father Dan Cambria of the Divine Mercy Chapel in New Orleans tells a different version of the story. According to Father Dan, it was the Ursuline nuns who received an unidentified statue just prior to the French Revolution. All over the exterior of the crate in which the statue was housed were the words **EXPEDITE.** The nuns proceeded to open up the box and when they saw the statue, none of them recognized who it was. They asked the bishop to identify the saint and the bishop was unable to do so. So, they wrote a letter to the people who sent the statue from France and inquired about its identity. Unfortunately, the French Revolution had already begun and they never received a reply. So, they placed the statue of the unidentified saint— whom they now called St Expedite—at the end of a corridor of their school where it remained for several decades.

St. Expedite, though located at the end of a corridor where he could have easily been forgotten was, in fact, not forgotten or ignored. The students living in the convent took a liking to him. They prayed to him

Statue of St. Expedite located in Our Lady of Guadalupe Chapel in New Orleans. Photo by Infrogmation, 2007 Wikimedia Commons. This file is licensed under the Creative Commons Attribution 2.0 Generic license.

and eventually developed what is referred to as the *Nine Hour Novena to St. Expedite*. Now, novenas are not uncommon in Catholicism; there are nine day novenas to virtually all saints. However, St. Expedite's novena was what is referred to as a *flying novena* because it is said for nine hours and according to this story, the students achieved positive results when praying to him in this manner. His devotion continued to grow among the student body and he gained the reputation for bringing unusually quick results to prayers.

Because Father Dan views this legend as a "light-hearted" story, he suggests the feast day for St. Expedite might be April 1st, April Fool's Day, as opposed to April 19th. Father Dan clearly does not recognize St. Expedite as an official saint in Catholicism; but, at least he concedes that when people pray to St. Expedite, they get results, and quick ones at that.

## The Denial of St. Expedite

Because of a paucity of written historical accounts of St. Expedite there has been an ongoing campaign by the Church to convince the Catholic world that St. Expedite is simply a figment of a universal collective imagination. There are reportedly no relics of his body, after all, except those associated with the story of his arrival in Réunion. It is as if he simply vanished after his beheading in 303. The church where he is housed in New Orleans, the Our Lady of Guadalupe Chapel, makes minimal reference to him on their website and there are reports from patrons of the gift shop there that when asked about St. Expedite, shopkeepers refuse to speak of him. Williams (2011), for example, reports this experience:

> My questions at the church and its adjacent gift shop went largely unanswered. The woman working at the gift shop claimed to know nothing of St. Expedite, although prayer cards, small statues, and medals all bore the image of the saint ... She not only refused to verify St. Expedite's authenticity but declined to speak about the saint at all. (Williams, 2011, par. 5, lines 1-16).

One of the primary reasons cited for denying St. Expedite's existence is the mistakes found in the Marytologies of Jerome. For example, CatholicOnline.com, though they include him as an entry in their database, has this to say about St. Expedite:

> At one time there was much talk of a Saint Expeditus, and some good people were led to believe that, when there was need of haste, petitioning Saint Expeditus was likely to meet with prompt settlement. However, there is no adequate reason to think that any such saint was ever invoked in the early Christian centuries; in fact, it is more than doubtful whether the saint ever existed. In the "Hieronymianum" the name Expeditus occurs among a group of martyrs both on the 18th and 19th of April, being assigned in the one case to Rome, and in the other to Melitene in Armenia; but there is no vestige of any tradition which would corroborate either mention, whereas there is much to suggest that in both lists the introduction of the name is merely a copyist's blunder. Hundreds of similar blunders have been quite definitely proved to exist in the same document. (http://www.catholic.org/saints/saint.php?saint_id=347).

This logic is perplexing to me. Why single out St. Expedite? Furthermore, where is the source of this proof of a "copyist blunder?" If the Martyrologies of St. Jerome are that unreliable, then shouldn't the entire thing be scrapped instead of focusing on a single saint?

The other primary reason for the denial of St. Expedite seems to be based on the popular word play attributed to the saint. According to CatholicOnline.com, "It should be pointed out that the recognition of St. Expeditus as the patron of dispatch depends beyond doubt upon a play upon words." Obviously, this play on words refers to both the origin stories of the crates marked **Expedite**, as well as his iconography. Before one completely dismisses the origin stories, however, it should be noted that in each case where there was the arrival of a crate marked "Expedite" and no other identifying information, there contained a statue of a Roman Centurion holding a cross with the word "hodie" inscribed on it and stomping on a crow with the word "cras" written on a ribbon held in the bird's beak. And as has already been pointed out, there are quite a few of these statues in a number of churches across the world.  If it is a hoax, then who has been sending these statues to churches all over the world for the last couple of hundred years?

In contrast to CatholicOnline.org, Catholicism.org takes one step forward in pointing out to the deniers that St Expeditus was indeed a real saint. Then, they take a predictable three steps back when discussing him with regards to his relationship with Voudou's Baron Samedi and Baron La Croix:

> It is well-known that several Catholic saints, including the Virgin Mary herself, have been adopted by believers in fetish-like cult religions, especially Haitian Voodoo, and some other African tribal fetishes that became established in the Caribbean islands... So it is with Saint Expedite. In New Orleans, among adherents of the Hoodoo magic, Saint Expedite represents to these practitioners, Baron Samedi, actually an evil spirit of the underworld. Followers of Haitian Voodoo venerate him as representing Baron Lakwa, also an evil spirit. The followers of these dark cults used Catholic saints to disguise their mysterious and occult beliefs and to give their ceremonies an air of legitimacy. (http://catholicism.org/patron-saint-for-the-impatient.html).

It is no secret that the Catholic Church has made numerous attempts to eradicate traditional African religions in the past. Even with the legal mandates of the Black codes which forbade any slaves (and anyone else, for that matter) to practice any religion other than Catholicism in Louisiana, however, these attempts proved to backfire on the Church. Sure, the laws may have forced everyone to be baptized Catholic or convert to Catholicism; but, it also gave the slaves a tool to continue their own religions by disguising African gods with Catholic saints. This process of associating one deity for another via a thinly-veneered substitution is called *syncretization*.

Admittedly, the puns, duplicate origin stories and so-called copyist blunders in the Martyrologies do little to legitimatize St. Expedite in the eyes of the Church or among skeptics. However, there is something to this saint, something that makes him recognized as a powerful spirit in many areas of the world. Could it be that everyone is delusional? Are all of the people who love and revere him as they do simply loving and revering a concept and a fictional saint?

Voudou has always been an inclusive religion in New Orleans out of necessity. The social conditions which forced people from different cultures to be in such close proximity with one another created an atmosphere of spiritual unity in a sense, and spirituality and the new hybrid religion fueled the resilience of the oppressed. Now, there are many Catholic saints as a part of New Orleans Voudou—there is no longer the need to hide behind the veil of Catholicism. Instead, practitioners embrace elements of Catholicism. And guess who is among those embraced? That's right, the ousted Minute Saint himself. Many thanks to the Catholic Church for this one.

The removal of St. Expedite from the liturgical calendar does not seem to have impacted the devotion practiced by those who love him, or the other saints removed, for that matter. St. Expedite is a major figure in both folk Catholic worship and Voudou in New Orleans, much to the chagrin of naysayers and deniers, and he has become quite popular among non-Catholic hoodoo and rootwork practitioners nationwide. No matter their background or religious persuasion, people are alike in the sense that if something works, why question it or deny it? The cult of St. Expedite's devotion among conjurers and regular folks only seems to be growing.

# St. Expedite and New Orleans Voudou

In New Orleans Voudou, St. Expedite is syncretized with the lwa Baron Samedi, the spirit of death, guardian of the cemeteries and head of the family of ancestral spirits called the Guede. In fact, some circles refer to Baron Samedi as St. Expedite almost as if the two are one and the same. For example, St. Expedite plays an important role in the opening ceremony of Mardi Gras. To the general public, Mardi Gras simply looks like a party in the streets—and indeed it is. However, there are much deeper mysteries at play that are related to Voudou that the average person is completely unaware of. Mardi Gras follows a specific procession, starting with the North Side Skull and Bones Gang who represent St. Expedite. According to Spiritualist Cinnamon Black with the New Orleans Voodoo Museum, "St. Expedite sits at the gates of the cemetery and comes alive at about 4:00 in the morning in Congo Square, here in New Orleans, where they practice a ritual and pray for the beginning of Mardi Gras" (Black, 2011).

The North Side Skull and Bones Gang is an obscure tradition that began in the early 1800s. They wake up at the crack of dawn on Mardi Gras morning and traverse around the Treme neighborhood yelling out a variety of disturbing phrases such as "The Worms Go In, The Worms Go Out," "You Next!" and "If You Don't Live Right, The Bone Man Is Comin' For Ya!" As they parade through the street, they knock on the doors of residents, spreading positive messages like "stay in school, "say no to drugs" and the like. The parents let them into their homes and they proceed to go to the children's bedrooms where they are awoken to the site of skeletons

*(Continued page 36)*

HODIE

don't procrastinate

Much Love!

EXIT!

D Alvarrado 2014

telling them to listen to their mamas or else, after which they say if you don't do these things you're going to die. Essentially, their overall message is the same as St. Expedite's: Do what you can today because tomorrow may not come. Procrastination be gone! In addition to Mardi Gras, St. Expedite leads the Skull and Bones for St Joseph's Day and Day of the Dead celebrations.

The infamous statue of St. Expedite in New Orleans is still located in Our Lady of Guadalupe Chapel on the right hand side, just inside the door. On the other side of the chapel is a statue of St Jude, Patron Saint of the Hopeless. There are a number of practices engaged in by locals and tourists alike that involves one or both of these statues. Prayers, offerings, and requests are made by visitors to the chapel in quite creative ways since the Missionary Oblates of Mary Immaculate, who maintain the Our Lady of Guadalupe chapel, do not allow devotees to leave offerings at the feet of the statues. So, Voudou devotees and Hoodoo practitioners will sometimes leave offerings for St. Expedite in the care of Marie Laveaux, whose famous tomb is located just a hop, skip and a jump away in St Louis Cemetery #1. It is believed that Marie Laveaux will accept gifts on behalf of St. Expedite for those who wish to compensate him for his services. People do manage to covertly leave written petitions in the chapel at his feet, however. Those who may be more straightforward Catholic in their beliefs will go to St. Jude and pray for his intercession, then head on over to the other side of the chapel and ask St. Expedite to make their request happen fast.

An early mention of St. Expedite in relationship to New Orleans Voudou was made in 1946 by Robert Tallant in his book, *Voodoo in New Orleans*. In the book, Tallant discusses St. Expedite as a "doubtful" saint, while at the same time confirming him as the "most dependable saint in Heaven when it comes to getting things done in a hurry" (Tallant, 1946, p. 205). Tallant also comments on the noncommittal attitude by priests towards St. Expedite. It seems the priestly attitude hasn't changed a bit; it's almost as if the perpetuation of the

## THE OLD MORTUARY CHAPEL

Built in 1826 as a burial church for victims of yellow fever, the chapel is oldest surviving church in the city. Now Our Lady of Guadalupe, the chapel is the official chapel of the New Orleans Police and Fire Departments.

urban legend is part of the St. Expedite tradition itself. According to Tallant:

Perhaps the popular saint in the Voodoo world is St. Expedite, who, incidentally, is a peculiar example of the bridge between New Orleans Voodooism and Catholicism. Though his authenticity is more than doubtful, statues of St. Expedite are in at least two Catholic churches in the city, one of them Our Lady of Guadalupe, which is situated on North Rampart Street, almost adjacent to St Louis Cemetery No. 1 and just around the corner from where the Laveaus lived. The church is a very old one and was originally the Catholic chapel from which all burial services were held. Both Maries must have known it well.

Priests, questioned about St. Expedite remain noncommittal. Some will tell you they are certain he did exist. Others disagree entirely. There are no records. Some years ago Archbishop Shaw of New Orleans made a public and angry demand that these statues be removed from Catholic churches in New Orleans. But nothing was ever done, and the statues remain, Since then, two Negro "Mothers" have opened St. Expedite temples.

But whatever the truth is about his history, many New

Orleanians know that St. Expedite is the most dependable saint in Heaven when it comes to getting things done in a hurry. You only have to say, "St. Expedite, do this now." It will be done. Then you go to his statue at Our Lady of Guadalupe Church and pay off—sometimes by burning a candle before him and saying a prayer, but other times, if you're a genuine Voodoo, by leaving a slice of pound cake, a new penny or a sprig of green fern at his feet. Such articles are constantly being found before the image. (Tallant, 1946, p. 205).

As much as I have criticized Tallant in the past for his embellished and oft inaccurate depictions of New Orleans Voudou, I have to admit that he is the only one I have found to report on the manner in which St. Expedite is utilized in uncrossing and for protection against gris gris. Whether or not the individual he spoke to actually existed or not is hard to say; nonetheless, the details in his descriptions of the type of gris gris used and how it was deployed is accurate, and the manner in which St. Expedite is called upon also appears authentic. For these reasons, I have reproduced his accounts below:

Octavia Williams believed that going to see St. Expedite was the best thing you could do if you found gris gris on your door step.

"He's the one that can do the fast work," she said. There is lots of ways you can keep from being hoodooed. You ought to always make a hole in a silver dime and paste a saint's picture on it and put it up on the transom of your front door when you move into a new house. But once you is gris grised, always call on St. Expedite for help.

"I done found salt on my steps one morning and right away I snapped my fingers and St. Expedite heard me. A woman across the street let out a scream and I found out later she had fallen off a ladder and broke her arm. She was the one who had tried to put a curse on me. You see how fast St. Expedite work?

"One time I was in my front yard and a man walk through the gate an' just stand there lookin' at me. I said, 'What you want? Don't stare at me that way.' But he kept lookin' at me and soon I felt I was getting' under his spell. 'Go get me a drink of water,' he say. Now, I ain't never refused a drink of water to man or beast so I went and got it. But when I came back he take the glass from my hand and don't say a word. He just hoodoo me some more wit' his eyes. I felt so funny. I knowed I was gonna do anything he asked me. 'Go inside and get your money and give it to me,' he say. And I went on in and came back wit' all the money I had in the world—about seventy dollars. I just couldn't help myself. I gave it to him and he asked me if that was all I had. I shook my head 'cause I couldn't hardly talk.

"Then something happen. That man turned around and started to walk off, and you know the minute he had turned his head something had broke the spell. All of a sudden I got my sense. I yell, "St. Expedite, help me now!" You won't believe this, but all of a sudden a two-by-four came flying through the air and that hunk of wood hit that thief on the head and knocked him cold. I grabbed my money out of his hand and start callin' my neighbors. They got the police, and that man is still in jail.

"Another time I done found a candle and a box of snuff on the doorstep and I knowed what that meant. I went inside the house and opened the pillow I slept on and inside I found a hoodoo thing—a lot of feathers tied with string and a piece of red wax in the middle. I had to dump the insides of every pillow I owned in the river. I called on St. Expedite the whole time I was doing this and then I went and burned a candle to him at Our Lady of Guadalupe Church. Wit' all that nothing' ever done happen to me. That proves how good that saint is, don't it?" (Tallant, 1946, pp. 205-207).

# Newspaper Articles about St. Expedite from 1896 and 1905

The following article is from the Evening Star, Washington D.C. and references a statue of St. Expedite being installed in a church there. It is dated March 28, 1896, page 7.

Miss Alice Riggs lately presented to St Matthew's new church a statue of St. Expedite, who is known as the saint of "today," and the one to whom intercession is made, in case of emergency. Devotion to St. Expedite has become widely spread in France and more lately in this country where he seems particularly to meet the hustling spirit of the day, which is not content to wait longer for its favors. St. Expedite was one of the early martyrs, and is represented holding a palm branch in one hand and a cross in the other, on which is inscribed the Latin word "Hodie" - "Today." One foot rests on a crow, which has a scroll in its beak and the inscription, "Cras." A literal and practical translation of this word almost reveals the old proverb, "Don't put off till tomorrow what you can do today."

The newspaper clipping on the right is unfortunately torn and in pretty bad shape, but it is the only one I could find so far about the decanonization of St. Expedite. In the torn areas, it references the origin story of St. Expedite in France when the nuns requested relics from the catacombs (see page 18). The rest is difficult to piece together, but it seems the last paragraph alludes to St. Expedite's legend as a hoax. The article is from the Blue-grass Blade, Lexington, Kentucky and is dated December 24, 1905.

## POPE DECANONIZES

### The Popular Neapolitan Saint Who Granted Prayers Too Expediously

Naples, December 9.— St. Expedito, a popular Neapolitan saint, whose specialty has been the too quick grant- ing of prayers, has been decanonized by the Pope, and the officials of the church in Naples have been ordered to remove his images from the places of worship.

It appears that the worship of St. Expedito rested on a misunderstand- ing. An Armenian martyr by that name is known to have existed, but he was not canonized. In the latter half of the nineteenth century some nuns begged that certain relics discovered in the catacombs migh_ be sent to ____ convent, and the Pope gave his ____sion to its being done.

____ase containing the bones was ____ "Expedit," and the good Sis- ____stook the directions for the ____ the saint to whom the r____.

—————

____nment—The above ____ ____ bones taken fr____ ____ere sent to Naple____ —which means I sup____ livered, expedity or wi____ ____tch. The nuns, ther____ ____ the ____ ____ pedito," which bones got ____ prayers so "expeditio____ good Pope Sarto ____ o____.

For an exposit____ were made, and n____ hoaxes like the above—see— to Rome."

The article below is from the *Tablet, the International Catholic News Weekly,* is credited to "Our own Correspondent" and appears in the Saturday November 4, 1905 edition, p. 17.

# CORRESPONDENCE.

### ROME.
#### (FROM OUR OWN CORRESPONDENT.)
Sunday, October 29, 1905.

## THE TRUTH ABOUT ST. EXPEDITUS.

A new Congregation of Rites has sprung up in quite an unexpected quarter this week, to wit in the columns of the daily press of Italy, Germany, and France. The editors have suddenly become exceedingly interested in the case of St. Expeditus. As might have been expected, most of the editors have not only uncanonised this Saint, but have sternly relegated him to the regions of myth and fable. Their interest in the Saint has been aroused by a report that the popular devotion to him in Rome is being discouraged by the Apostolic Visitors, and that his statue has been removed from some of the churches in which it formerly occupied a prominent position. The real truth is that in some places and among some people devotion to St. Expeditus has taken an eccentric and exaggerated form. It seems to have started in Austria about the middle of the 18th century, and it is now very common in most European countries. St. Expeditus is invoked as the patron of urgent cases—he is depicted as a Roman soldier, holding in his right hand a cross on which is inscribed the word "To-day," and crushing with his foot a crow which is just able to croak out the word "To-morrow." The symbolism is quite modern, and has struck many devout Catholics as somewhat ridiculous. In the popular mind it is supposed to mean that St. Expeditus obtains for you without delay any favours you ask through his intercession. Doubtless the name "Expeditus" has given rise to this belief, but it has received currency and strength through the medium of popular "lives" of the Saint which are nothing better than a tissue of the idlest conjecture. All we know with certainty of St. Expeditus is summed up in the two facts that he existed in an early period of Christianity and that he was martyred; these are quite sufficient to entitle him to the veneration of Catholics, but they certainly afford no justification for the countless stories which are related of him or for the picture of him which has become so popular. It is not true that the Apostolic Visitors of Rome have been authorised to abolish all devotion to this holy martyr, but it is more than probable that they are quietly reducing it to its proper sphere and limits.

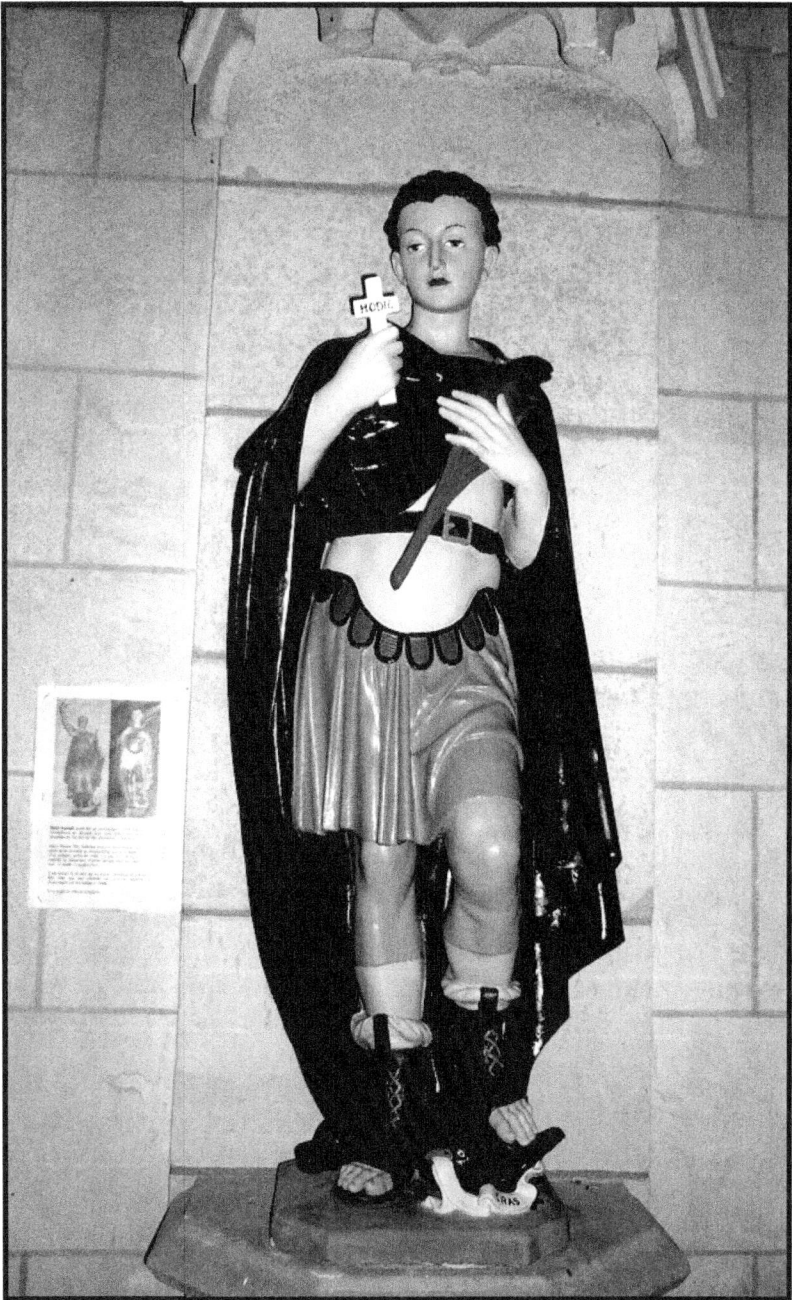

Statue of St. Expedite in the Church of Our Lady of the Assumption in Montbert, France. Photo © Jimmy NICOLLE, CC-BY-SA, Wikimedia Commons.

# Patronage and Attributes

**Feast day:** April 19
**Patronage:** Emergencies, procrastinators, merchants, navigators, computer programmers, hackers, revolutionaries, examinees, anyone needing a quick solution to a problem, ecommerce, internet users, New Orleans, Republic of Molossia
**Birth:** Unknown
**Death:** 303
**Canonization:** Martyrdom by Diocletian in Armenia (beheaded)
**Day of the week:** Wednesday, Thursday, Friday
**Candle color:** All colors, especially red, green, yellow, pink, blue, white, black, red/green double action candles
**Offerings:** Sara Lee pound cake, red and green flowers, water, candles, red rock salt, red wine, white rum, milk, Cajun and Creole spices, green vegetables, palm, green herbs, rain water
**Payment for Services Rendered:** pound cake, candles, flowers, charitable work, giving money to the poor, public acknowledgement
**Petition:** when haste in any matter is needed; for fast solutions to problems; when your computer is not cooperating; for better business; when taking a test or exam; for finances; to end procrastination; for love; for money; healing; court cases; law suits; cursing an enemy; death, dying, and sorcery (these latter left-handed petitions are not part of traditional Catholic devotion to St. Expedite)
**Corresponding Voudou/Vodou Lwa:** Baron Samedi, Baron LaCroix, Guede Limbo

# CHAPTER 2:
# WORKING WITH ST. EXPEDITE
### Setting up his Altar, Magickal Pound Cake & a Note to Pagans, Wiccans & NonCatholics

When working with St. Expedite within the context of conjure, it is difficult to divorce him completely from Catholicism. Even though he is not recognized as an official Catholic saint, his influence in the lives of many practicing Catholics as well as nonCatholics, hoodoos, rootworkers, and Voudouists cannot be discounted.

There are a few basic things to remember when working with St. Expedite. First and foremost, use common courtesy. Consider how you would feel if a stranger came up to you and asked for a slew of favors without saying please and thank you. He doesn't have to help you if he doesn't want to. Remember, you are the one in need of a favor, not the other way around. So, be polite.

Secondly, devotees of St. Expedite tend to stress asking him only for positive reasons and never for anything that will cause harm to another person. This is true for all official Catholic saints and folk saints if praying with them in the context of Catholicism. That said, there are some people who tend to energize the shadow side of spirits and enjoy working with those energies for nefarious reasons. These are the folks who will petition St. Expedite to put a curse on someone or even to cause the death of someone. This type of work is related to St. Expedite's syncretization with Baron Samedi, who is a powerful sorcerer and can both dispense and counter any black magic. So, how he is invoked is dependent upon the religiomagical context in which he is situated.

Third, there are some basic guidelines to follow when

working with St. Expedite. While these general rules are not necessarily universal practices, they are effective guidelines for people beginning to work with him and who are still getting to know him. To increase the chances of your success when working with St. Expedite, keep these thing in mind:

- Develop a relationship with him. Celebrate his feast day every year and on the 19th of each month. Say a daily devotional to him without asking for anything. Choose one of the prayers in this book to get started.
- If praying a novena, pray for nine days and stop. If you keep praying the novena beyond the nine days, he will think you are continuing to ask him for help and he may not do so until you stop. Follow the instructions in this book for praying a novena successfully.
- If praying a Triddum, pray the Triduum for three days then stop. The same principle holds as for praying a novena. Pray the Triduum, and make your request Then stop, and let him answer.
- Have the offerings you promise him on hand. He should be offered his reward for helping ASAP, within the hour if at all possible.
- Set up an altar dedicated to him.
- Only ask him for one favor at a time.
- Be specific with your request If you need $600.00, state you need $600.00 by a certain date.
- Be respectful.
- Turn his image upside down when petitioning him and keep him that way until he grants your request
- Do not turn his image upside down if you are making a simple devotional to him.
- Don't forget to pay him for his help. And, be sure it is what you promised him. Do not substitute red wine for white rum. Do not substitute cookies for Sara Lee pound cake.
- Do not pay him until after he has granted your request.
- Do not forget to honor him publicly after he has helped

you. Take out an ad in the local newspaper or in the Hoo-doo Almanac, make a public declaration on a forum or social networking site, or on his blog: http://saint-expedite.blogspot.com.

- If you do not follow through with your end of the deal, be prepared for him to take back everything he has given. He is a kind and generous saint, but he is no doormat. A deal is a deal, renege on your part and be prepared for the consequences.

## Setting Up his Altar

St. Expedite's altar is set up in a triangle pattern. Modern practitioners tend to use red candles when working with St. Expedite; but, any color can be used with him and of course the staple white candle is always an ideal substitute. Some basic guidelines (not set in stone) include petitioning St. Expedite on Wednesdays with red candles, Thursdays with yellow candles and Fridays with green candles. You can use a glass encased candle with his image on it, a votive candle, taper candle, an offertory candle or even a tea light. Whichever candle you use, place it at the back of the altar; this is the tip of the triangle formation. In the front and to the left, place an ordinary glass of water or rain water if you can get it and in the front and to the right of the triangle place the statue or image of him in the form of a picture or holy card.

In hoodoo, it is customary to offer St. Expedite pound cake, flowers, and a glass of water. In New Orleans, he is typically offered Sara Lee pound cake, but homemade pound cake is equally as good. He is believed to grant any request within his power provided the petitioner recommends his invocation to others. Offerings are best made after requests are granted. The reason offerings are made after he grants his request is because it is payment for his services—an incentive if you will. If you pay him beforehand, he has no incentive to work quickly on your behalf.

Once his altar is set up and you are ready to petition him, turn his image upside down. If you are making a simple devo-

(Continued on page 50)

Candle

Glass of Water

Image of St Expedite

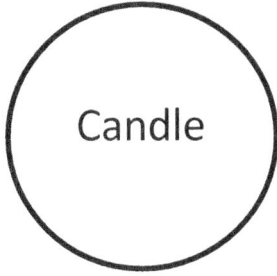

Basic Altar configuration for St. Expedite in the shape of a triangle. His image is turned upside down when a work commences and turned right side up once a petition is answered.

tional, this is not necessary; but, if you are invoking his intercession for a favor to be granted, turning his image upside down signifies a work is in progress. Then, ring the bell three times while calling out his name. This is to wake him up and get his attention. If you do not have a silver bell, tap on the glass of water three times or knock on the altar table three times while calling his name. Then, proceed with any of the works and prayers in the next sections of the book. When he answers your petition, be sure to set him right side up again and give him public praise and a piece of pound cake. Do not eat the offerings you have given him. After 24 hours, throw the offerings outside under a tree and let the birds or other animals eat them. If you have given him white rum, leave it on his altar until it is consumed.

## St. Expedite's Magickal Pound Cake

The classic ritual food offering to St. Expedite is pound cake. In New Orleans, it is Sara Lee pound cake that has become tradition, Most likely because it is cheap, easy to get, and for a few bucks you can keep a loaf in the freezer ready to pull out and slice off a piece at a moment's notice.

The second best thing to Sara Lee pound cake is homemade pound cake. It is easy to make and you can make some for yourself. The ingredients lend themselves to a very magickal pound cake, with luck drawing ingredients like sugar and vanilla, lemon to clear away blockages, and eggs and flour to bring abundance. In fact, the ingredients of pound cake reflect well the gifts St. Expedite has the ability to bring his devotees. But, pound cake is not limited to loafs. You can get creative with your pound cakes if you are an avid baker. You can make pound cake balls, pound cakes with pudding filling, bundt cakes, layered pound cakes, and swirled pound cakes, for example.

The following recipe is from the cook book, *The New Royal Cook Book*, which was published in 1920 and is in the public domain.

## Ingredients
- 1 cup butter  (brings wealth and prosperity)
- 1 cup sugar (to sweeten what's coming)
- 1 teaspoon vanilla extract (for attraction)
- 1 teaspoon lemon extract (cut through obstacles and clear the way)
- 5 eggs (for growth and abundance)
- 2 cups flour (for abundance)
- 1 teaspoon Royal Baking Powder (to help you rise to your potential)
- Reserve 2 egg whites for icing (for the proverbial icing on the cake)

## Directions
Cream butter and sugar, beating well. Add flavoring and egg yolks which have been beaten until pale yellow. Beat three egg whites until light and add alternately a little at a time with the flour which has been sifted with baking powder. Mix well and bake in greased loaf pan in moderate oven about one hour. Cover with ornamental frosting, made with the two remaining egg whites.

# Ornamental Frosting
## Ingredients
- 1-1/2 cups granulated sugar
- 1/2 cup water
- 2 egg whites
- 1 teaspoon flavoring extract
- 1 teaspoon Royal Baking Powder

## Directions
Boil sugar and water without stirring until syrup spins a thread; add very slowly to beaten egg whites. Add flavoring and baking powder, beat until smooth and stiff enough to spread. Put over boiling water, stirring continually until icing grates slightly on bottom of bowl. Spread on cake, saving a small portion of icing to ornament the edge of cake.

# A Note to Pagans, Wiccans & NonCatholics

I am often asked by Pagans, Wiccans and nonCatholics if they are able to work with St. Expedite, and if they can do so without using Catholic prayers. Here are some of my thoughts about this issue.

While St. Expedite comes out of the Catholic tradition, he has been pushed to the fringe by the religion itself through no fault of his own. In my opinion, this makes him available to people from other traditions who wish to embrace him, such as Voudou and folk Catholicism, for example. I find it difficult to divorce him completely from Catholicism, however. To work with him without his prayers would be stripping his core tradition from him and that doesn't feel right to me. There is a workaround however, that keeps him within the structure in which he is grounded; yet, also places him in a meaningful context for Pagans, Wiccans, and nonCatholics.

The main issue seems to be the wording of the prayers. Therefore, this is where the adaptation can occur. It is no secret that Catholicism and Christianity borrowed heavily from Pagan traditions, so to substitute the word "Goddess" for "Mary" or "Holy Mother" is not a stretch. Also, St. Expedite came out of a Roman pagan background before converting to Christianity. You may try substituting Roman pagan gods or Lord and Lady for lines in prayers that call for "God" and "Jesus." In other words, whoever your Highest divinity is, whoever is the God/Goddess of your understanding, substitute their names where appropriate. Or, leave it out altogether. While I cannot guarantee he will respond to you, I cannot say he will not either. You will have to experiment and figure it out for yourself.

One thing I can say about working with any saint or Spirit is that you must develop a relationship with them. So start there. Set up a shrine for St. Expedite and begin to talk to him daily. Write your own prayers that are heartfelt and meaningful to you. Once you have done this, he is far more likely to answer any petitions for help, whatever your religious persuasion or spiritual path may be.

HODIE

2012

# CHAPTER 3:
# THE HYATT TEXTS
## The Minute Saint from Court Scrapes to Sorcery

This section focuses on working with St. Expedite through conjure and prayer, and in the context of New Orleans Voudou, folk Catholicism and Hoodoo. To begin, I devote a section of information found in Harry Middleton Hyatt's (1973) seminal work, *Hoodoo-Conjuration-Witchcraft-Rootwork.* I have studied all of the entries about him in all five volumes and through a methodological approach, developed categories of workings for which St. Expedite was invoked by informants. It sets the tone for the next chapter of practical conjures.

In Chapter 4, I provide a section of practical conjures of my own, as well as others I developed that were inspired by my research. Thus, there will be much in that chapter that is new to the reader-practitioner, simply because it has never been made public before. Information in this chapter will be new to folks who do not have access to the Hyatt texts due to their limited availability and high cost. If you have read the entire book up to this point, the workings themselves should make sense to you. If not, go back and read the beginning of the book to get familiar with St. Expedite's background and how he is served and petitioned in different areas of the world.

Be prepared to find information that may not jive with what you are used to hearing about St. Expedite. Keep an open mind as much of this comes from the old-timers who worked with him long before many readers of this book were born. In observing a tradition, it is important to take as broad and deep a look as possible; hopefully, I have accomplished that here.

# St. Espidee in the Hyatt Texts

*"Now, St Espidee, he keeps yore enemies down—he's got his feet on de pigeon, see, an' he's fo' landlords, but he don't want no prayin' tuh him. Yo' axe St Espidee whut chew wants an' he'll give it to yo', if yo' don't pray to him."* ~ Informant 1579, Algiers, Louisiana

Aside from the minimal references to St. Expedite found in the Christian martyrologies, a few newspaper articles, the brief mentions in Ray Malbrough's (2003) *Hoodoo Mysteries* and Alfred Metraux's (1959) *Voodoo,* there are some references to St. Expedite in Harry Middleton Hyatt's (1973) 5 Volume set *Hoodoo-Conjuration-Witchcraft-Rootwork.* In that work, informants refer to him as *St. Expedite, St Espidee, Espidy, Espedees* and *'Spedee,* along with a few other variations. Why the transcriber did not spell the name consistently when possible is beyond me and makes for doing research in the texts challenging, to say the least. In any event, the manner in which he is described and the works reported are consistent with current popular thought of using predominantly red candles, working with him on Wednesdays, and petitioning him for quick results. On the other hand, there are some significant departures from today's norm. For example, he is also petitioned with a variety of different colored candles for court scrapes, getting a job, quick money, making wishes, gambling, conquering enemies, banishing, opening roads and sorcery, for example. There are also references regarding how he is placed, such as on the floor, rightside up or upside down, and practices of rapping, finger snapping or ringing a bell to get his attention when invoking his intercession.

An interesting practice that was shared among informants is the sending of someone before St. Expedite to announce his coming or to make the way for him (*"get in de lead"*), and to send someone after him to make sure he does the job he is sent to do. We see this in New Orleans Voudou where Baron

Samedi is often sent after St. Expedite to insure the work is accomplished. Typically, it is the Holy Trinity or God who is invoked first to make the way for St. Expedite; in New Orleans, it is often Our Lady of Guadalupe. This practice is shared in the context of hoodoo in the Hyatt texts and is not identified with the Voudou religion by any of the informants, nor was Hyatt apparently aware it actually comes from a religious practice. Thus, the connection to Voudou regarding this particular practice of sending a spirit before and after a saint is not made in by Hyatt in his 5 volume work.

Once you read the following examples and excerpts from the Hyatt texts, it should become clear as to how you may work with St. Expedite yourself. Using some of the techniques the old-timers used will likely enhance your personal relationship with St. Expedite. You will find in the conjures that follow this section I have done just that for some of the works I created. Hopefully, they will inspire you to create your own original conjures, as well.

Note that in the following excerpts, Hyatt's comments and questions are enclosed in quotation marks and the informant's comments are italicized. This is done for better readability and to differentiate my comments from those of Hyatt's and the informants'.

## The Saint of Many Colors

In the Hyatt texts, one informant refers to St. Expedite as the *Saint of Many Colors*. She calls him this based on the fact that his clothing is very colorful. In fact, this color association between saints and their clothing and the color of candle used, is observed with other saints, as well. For example, St. Anthony wears a brown robe so his candle color is brown. St. Jude wears a green robe, so his candle color is green. If you are ever in doubt about what color candle to use with a particular saint, look at their iconography and observe the color of the clothing they are wearing. Use the predominant color as the primary color. Of course, a white candle can always be used with any saint whenever petitioning them for any purpose.

The name of the conjure doctor who shared the information about using many different candle colors with St Espidee was called "Nahnee." Nahnee was from Algiers, Louisiana and called herself the "Boss of Algiers." She basically stated that a petition begins with a red candle on the first day, which is allowed to burn down. Then, a green candle is lit the next day and allowed to burn down. The following day, a yellow candle is lit and allowed to burn down. A different color candle is burned every day for nine days to petition St Espidee, the Saint of Many Colors. Note that she refers to candles as "lights."

*Now, yo' take—St Espidee is a saint of many colors, see. Now, today yo'll burn a red light, tomorrah yo'll burn a green light, tomorrah a yellah light. He wus a young Italian man an' he wus a saint of many colors.*

(How do you mean a saint of many colors?)

*A saint of many colors—dat chew have tuh use all colors tuh him—all colors—use a red light, a green light, a brown light—yo' use diff'rent lights, yo' see, each day.*

*Well, St Espedee works very quickly. His light is a red light on a Wednesday. He's fo' close scrapes—he's fo' quick money. But then there is a call behin' him. Somebody must go behin' St Espedee. He takes unless yo' give him flowers. Yo' must give him flowers because if not, then someone out the house will pass on.*

(What do you mean that he is a saint of many colors?) [I repeat my question and get a logical answer.]

*Dat mean he wo' many colors in his garments—many colors on his garments. Dat why yo' use many diff'rent lights— red, yellah, green, blue. Each day he gits a diff'rent color light fo' nine days. An' each time yo' light a light in front of dat lamp, yo' ring dat bell an' yo' make dat wish, an' dat party will wander off an' yo' won't know whut become of 'em.* (Nahnee, "The Boss of Algiers" Algiers, La., Vol. 2, p. 1373).

Although Nahnee doesn't go into any details about the lamp she is referring to, in New Orleans Voudou and Haitian Vodou, it is common practice to light a candle in front of an oil lamp (charm lamp, magick lamp) in order to activate it. Most rootworkers today will only use the candle itself or the lamp itself, but not both in combination. This practice is but one of several that can be found as a Voudou practice but never identified as such in the Hyatt texts. To see how this idea can be applied to working with a charm lamp, see the *Magick Lamp to Get a Job* on page 103 in the next section of *Practical Conjures*.

Another departure from the usual red candle color is shared by the informant Hyatt calls a *Woman and her Three Saints* from New Orleans. She describes using pink and blue candles with St. Expedite for love. She explains that blue candles are for truth and pink is for love, so burning a blue and a pink candle together will bring true love. I love this use of the two candle colors towards a specific goal.

*You burn a pink candle and a blue candle to St. Expedite. That's for love, true love, and for what you want—in asking him for money and things, for true things, for him to do truthful for you. You burn blue or pink to him.* (New Orleans, La. [872], Vol. 2 p. 1406).

## The Minute Saint

Just like everywhere else St. Expedite is known and celebrated, the old-timers in the Hyatt texts acknowledge him for his gift of rapidity. He's petitioned for quick solutions to all sorts of problems; one informant, Ida Bates, even stated she simply snaps her fingers to petition him. Talk about instant gratification!

*St. Expedite is a good saint. He's a quick saint, the minute saint.*

(What do you mean by that?)

*In three days he'll get a success. That's if you go with all your heart and mind and means what you say* (Ida Bates, 1938, New Orleans, La. Vol. 2, p. 1654).

*St Expedite is good. St. Expedite give you work. He'll open the way for you. He'll make your husband be good to you, if he's mean—if you pray to him. You pray to St. Expedite for work, money—ask him to help you, open the way for you. He'll give it to you—he'll do that. He'll give you anything you ask him for.*

## The Wishing Saint

St. Expedite is often referred to in the Hyatt texts as the saint to go to for making wishes. Wishes are made to him for any number of things, including gambling, food and money needs. Here, an informant from New Orleans describes how you would know if St. Expedite has heard your petition and whether or not he will answer your wish.

(Do you know anything about St. Espidy?)

*Well, St. Espidy, he's very good. He have helped me. He*

*helps me an' when ah wants bread ah call on him an' he brings me a rap [answers by rapping]. Ah heard dat he wus a man dat didn't believe in no evil work, an' he didn't fool roun' wit no kinda evil doin' when he wus on dis scene an' he wus a true man, an' when he died he went tuh heaven.*

(Now when he raps back, would he rap three times?)

*He jes' raps* [she demonstrates three times in diminishing volume].

(Where will he rap—somewhere around the room?)

*Yes.*

(Then you know you'll have your wish?)

*Yes.* (New Orleans, La. [1558], Vol. 1, p. 864).

## St. Espidee for Court Scrapes & Lawsuits

St. Expedite is called upon quite frequently for *court scrapes*, a term that refers to legal issues involving court appearances. He is relied on for court issues so much that he is even referred to as a lawyer by one informant from Algiers:

(St. Espidee is what?)

*Is a lawyer. Dat's a case of co't too. Well dey use de candles fo' him an' pray tuh him an' give him a glass of milk if yo' kin give it, or git white rum, an' give him yore case an' he'll plead it fo' yo'. Light a candle an' a glass of milk, or eithah yore rum if yo' kin git it, but yo' cain't git no mo' rum now.*

(What kind of color would you light to him?)

*A white one to St. Espidee.*

(What do you do, put him on the floor, too?)

*No, no—yo' leave him right up. He's gotta git up on de stand an' he's gotta talk fo' yo'.* (Algiers, La., [1584], Vol. 1, p. 865).

Note that this informant mentions offering St. Expedite milk or white rum and lighting a white candle for his help. Milk given as an offering to St. Expedite is not something I have ever seen or heard of outside of this entry by Hyatt. Now that's not to say it wasn't or isn't a common offering; only that I have not encountered it before. Putting milk and rum together however, would make a fabulous offering to St. Expedite: the traditional New Orleans libation of *Ponche aut lait* or *milk punch* calls for a blend of milk, rum or brandy, and sugar poured over crushed ice or served hot with a sprinkling of nutmeg or cinnamon on top for good measure (are you salivating yet?). Seriously though, the informant's emphasis on the difficulty of getting any rum is perhaps a cautionary move on the part of the informant. At the time of the Hyatt interviews, the country was on the tail end of the prohibition on alcohol (1919-1933) and it would have been quite fresh in her mind. That said, New Orleans was one of the leading suppliers of illegal alcohol during the prohibition, with home breweries amounting to at least three on every block. According to Ned Hémard from the New Orleans Bar Association, "As the apparent permanence of Prohibition sank in, the citizens of New Orleans (as well as the rest of the nation) had to seek alcohol through bootleggers or speakeasies. And in New Orleans, that task was not difficult" (Hémard, 2013, p.

*St Espidee's fine, he works fast He'll run yuh an' he'll bring yuh an' he'll do anythin'. If yo' promise 'im, yo give it to 'im. An' jis' pray an' ask 'im tuh do what yo' want. He works fast.*

5). This social atmosphere is one reason we find so many Law Keep Away works and works for Court Scrapes coming out of New Orleans hoodoo.

Next, we have an example of using a pink candle when petitioning "St. Expadee" for law suits. Note, this is yet another spelling of St. Expedite's name by Hyatt as an attempt to document African American colloquial speech that makes his research even more cumbersome to analyze.

*Saint Expadee—see, he's the conker in law suits.*

(How do you handle that?)

*Well you go to a Catholic church and you make your novena there, you see. You give a light. You take his picture and have it blest at the church and bring it to your house and you burn a pink candle to it all the time. Whatever you wish for, you prays to that saint and make your wishes and burn [a candle to] that saint—like if you got a case in court and you wanta conker that case. Well, you go to St. Expadee—go to the church and go to St. Expadee and make your novena to him and tell him what you want him to do. Then you come back home after you do that and you burn your candle at your home up until that case is over.*

[While machine is stopped, I ask question about his picture.]

*No, you don't bring his picture to the church, you always keep it in your house. You have his picture blest at the church and bring it to your house and have your little altar made and burn a pink candle to him.* (New Orleans, La., [851], Vol. 1, p. 866).

## St. Expedee for Law Keep Away

This next informant provides an interesting work, again using a pink candle, to keep away the police. Basically, an image of St. Expedite is hung above the door; typically, this means behind the front door and then a pink candle is lit behind the door to keep the police away.

*Git St. Expedee up over your door—nail him up over there. Behind that same door you use that pink candle, burn it there.*

*(Up over the door and behind the same door you burn a pink candle?)*

*Yes sir, and make your wishes. That's to keep the police away. It will keep 'em away.*

*(What door do you use for that?)*

*Let that be the front door.* (New Orleans, La., Vol. 6, pp. 864 -865).

*St Espidee is fo' gamblers. Yo' take St Espidee an' yo' gives him anything green, candle or flowers—green flowers or green vegetable. Anything dat is green, yo' give it to St Espidee fo' money. He's fo' gamblers .*

## St. Espidee to Bring a Man Back

There's no reason to believe St. Expedite shouldn't be petitioned for relationship issues, particularly in cases where a lover is strayed or wandered off. Petitioning him for such conditions is documented in the following passage:

*Yo' write yore name, de husban's name—yore name at de top an' his underneat' three times, but all straight. Dat's behin' St. Espidee cause ah have did it an' bring de man back. But chew use 'cordin' tuh his color, yore light to St. Espidee, an' he will bring dat man back. Jes' git down an' pray tuh him, "In de Name of de Father, de Son an' de Holy Spirit, St. Espidee, bring sich-an'-sich-a-one back," wit his name wrote behin' dat picture dat's tacked up—back of it pasted up dere. An' de man will come. An' keep dat light to him an' he goin' bring him back.*

(You put his name behind the picture?)

*Behin' dat picture.* (New Orleans, La., [1568], Vol. 1, p. 866).

## St. Espedee for Getting a Job

Not surprisingly, St. Expedite is reported by Hyatt informants to be invoked for job interviews and employment. In quite a few examples, there is the road opening aspect that is emphasized, including the deployment of God, the Holy Spirit or the Holy Trinity first to help open the way for St. Expedite to do the work he is asked to do.

*Well, St. Espedee, I knows about him. Now he's a good sent [saint]. He delivers zhoo, too. Jis' like if you wants a job—or somepin like that—he'll open a way fer you, if you believes in 'im, an' if you don't, well it's jis' like anything else.* [New Orleans, La., [787], Vol. 1 , p. 865].

This next informant from Algiers asks God to "git in de lead" of St. Expedite in order to secure a job:

*To speak to a boss yo' read the 23rd psalm and yo' git down and yo' pray befo' yo' goes an' ask God tuh git in de lead an ask him to sen' de spirit (St. Expedite) ahead of yo' tuh make a way fo' when yo' git dere dat dis man will speak tuh yo'.* (Algiers, La., Vol. 3 p. 1904)

## St. Expedite for Road Opening

St. Expedite's role as a road opener is quite pronounced in the Hyatt texts. One documented practice, for example, is described by an informant in New Orleans that is consistent with a road opening rite (the whole interview with the informant is provided on page 68). Take an image of St. Expedite and nail him right inside the front door. Offer St. Expedite a small toy hammer and a nail, and burn a black candle and red tapers to him and if someone has burned a candle on you, this will reportedly clear the way for you to continue living your life unencumbered by maleficent conjure.

Another ritual is described in association with getting a job:

> Now, St Espidee, he keeps yore enemies down - he's got his feet on de pigeon, see, an' he's fo' landlords, but he don't want no prayin' tuh him. Yo' axe St Espidee whut chew wants an' he'll give it to yo', if yo' don't pray to him.

> *St. Expedite is good. St. Expedite give you work. He'll open the way for you. He'll make your husband be good to you, if he's mean—if you pray to him. You pray to St. Expedite for work, money—ask him to help you, open the way for you. He'll give it to you—he'll do that. He'll give you anything you ask him for* (New Orleans, La. [872], Vol. 2, p 1406).

## St. Espidee for Luck and Success

Of course, it comes as no surprise that St. Expedite is petitioned for good luck and success, particularly in business ventures. In these cases, the informants emphasize the importance of keeping any promise made to him.

> *St. Espidee is fo' luck an' St. Espidee is fo' unfortunates. Lak if a man is unfortunate, well fo' luck he kin burn a candle.*

*Dey got cup candles dey call 'em. Dey sell dam in cups. Yo' burn a light tuh him eight days. Yo' burn a light tuh St. Espidee eight days an' yo' have some kinda luck in eight days, but dat's providin' if yo' make a promise to him. If yo' make a promise to him fo' luck an' success, he goin' give it to yo'; but if yo' lie to him, he'll take yore success away from yo'. Well, dat's de candle burnt to him dey call de cup candle, an' dat's whut he's fo', luck an' success.* (New Orleans, La., (1572), Vol. 1, p. 865).

(What do they say about St. Expedite?)

*Well, they say St. Expedite is lucky, but you gotta pray to him—certain things you gotta give to him for luck. You got ta have him up in your house and have a little altar-like and burn them little tapers to him for luck. Well, if you make him a promise or any thing and don't give it to him, well you falls in bad luck* (New Orleans, La., [845], Vol. 1 p. 866).

## St. Espedees for Gambling

As the saint of rapidity, St. Expedite lends himself perfectly to gamblers and those who enjoy playing games of chance.

*I tell you the saints—they have mighty good saints for the wishes that you wish. They have St. Espedees.*

(What is he for?)

*For a gambler.*

(Well, what would a gambler do for him?)

*Well, you see, if you gambling out for money and you're in bad luck, you goes there and you make a novena for nine days; and if you get your wishes, you gotta give it. If it's a dollar you promise, you have gotta give the dollar to it; if's a candle, a dollar candle light you have to give it to him.* (I see.)

*Then you get your wishes* (New Orleans, La., [874], Vol. 1 p. 865).

Likewise in Algiers, another informant states St. Expedite is for gamblers:

*St. Espidee is fo' gamblers. Yo' take St. Espidee an' yo' gives him anything green, candle or flowers—green flowers or green vegetable. Anything dat is green, yo' give it to St. Espidee fo' [green] money. He's fo' gamblers.*

*They pray to—wait, I'll tell you the saint to pray to to put 'em in bad luck—Expedee. Uh huh, that'll put choo in bad luck. Yes, sir.*

(How, how do you approach him?)

*Well, if yo'd go tuh him, yo' prays when yo' go tuh him an' yo'd ask him, say, "St Espidee ah want chew tuh help me tuh git some money. Ah'm goin' out an' gamble an' if ah be successful an' git dis money, ah will give yo' a bunch of flowers. Or give yo' so much an' so much of somepin green. Ah take de money an' buy it an' give it to yo'. "When yo' gits dis money yo' go tuh some church, or if yo' got him in yore house, yo' buys de stuff an' yo' puts it in front of him fo' a sacrifice* (Algiers, La., (1577), Vol. 1 p. 865).

## St. Espidee the Banisher

Similar to Voudou, St. Expedite is often reported to be petitioned to send people away.

*Well, St. Espidee, he's fo' - lak if yo' wanta send a person off, if yo' wanta work it lak dat. Well, yo' git St Espidee an' yo' git a silvah bell—one dose little small bells, little play bells, silvah bell, an' yo' place dat bell in de front of St Espidee's pitchure, wit de name of dat individual three times dat chew wanta wander off—send' em off. Yo' see.*

(What do you put that name on? )

*On a piece of papah, if it's a white person, yo' use a white papah an' red ink an' yo' write dat name three times; if it's a colored person, yo' take a little strip of brown papah an' yo' write de name three times wit black ink an' yo' place it right befo' St. Espidee. Now, yo' place it—heah's de silvah bell an 'heah's de name* [demonstrates].

(The silver bell is right in front of his picture, and the name is upon the bell.)

*Yessuh* (Algiers, La., Nahnee, "The Boss of Algiers," Vol. 2, p. 1373).

## St. Expedee the Two-Headed Saint

A little discussed aspect of St. Expedite is his association with sorcery. As already mentioned, this association with black magic and death conjure appears to be due to his association with Baron Samedi and New Orleans Voudou and Haitian Vodou. While none of the informants in the Hyatt texts make this verbal association, it is interesting in that it is perhaps a Voudou practice that the informants were either unaware of or did not want to mention. St. Expedite is treated by many as a two-headed saint, meaning, he is petitioned for harms and cures.

Hyatt asks an informant in Volume 2 (pp.1373-1374): "St Espidee will do any kind of work—evil work?"

The informant responds, "Yes—in de line of sending off or wanderin' a person away, or send a person off from a place dat chew don't want' em at, yo' understand."

Hyatt: "That's his specialty?

Informant: "Yes."

This next particular passage discusses burning a black candle to St. Expedite to bring someone bad luck.

St Raymond's for lucky things, but St. Expedee ain't. He's for devilment.

*They pray to—wait, I'll tell you the saint to pray to to put 'em in bad luck— Expedee. Uh huh, that'll put choo in bad luck. Yes, sir.*

(Suppose I want to put somebody in bad luck. What would I do?)

*Well, you go there [to a public hoodoo shrine] and you pray and you light a black can'le to 'er, you see, an' ask 'er what choo want, choo see. And then at nine days, if it's success, zhoo go back and you give'r whut zhoo promised 'er.*

(You only pray once , though? )
[My question means, you pray once when you set the candle, but you do not pray again during the nine days. She does not understand my question.]

*No.* [The candle is her prayer.] *Well, you kin put 25 cents in the box and that'll carry that light 9 days—you see, for that one light 25 cents in any Catholic church.*

[She is confusing the situation here. I do not think deliberately. She is obviously not a Roman Catholic—you do not buy a black candle in the Roman Catholic Church. But she knows a light can be set for a certain number of days.] (New Orleans, La., [814], Vol. 1 p. 866).

I would like to point out two things here with this informant. This is the second case where I observed an informant referring to St. Expedite as "her." This could be in reference to Our Lady of Guadalupe, who is often sent before St. Expedite in a petition. Also, Hyatt points out in his comments above (in brackets) that "she knows a light can be set for a certain number of days." She also apparently knows that black candles are burned to St. Expedite for nefarious reasons, whether or not she personally has done so, it seems to be common knowledge among informants who work with saints.

Following an interview where an informant refers to Black Hawk as one of the devil's servants, another informant discusses burning a black candle to St. Expedite to counter black magic:

*After they get the—after they burn that candle good on you [if someone is burning a candle against you], you go to this yere, this saint they call—you know a saint they call Expedite saint?*

(St. Expedite? No.)

*Uh-huh. You go to Expedite saint and you carry Expedite saint a little small kind of—go to the Ten Cent Store and you get you a small hammer; not no big hammer, a little toy hammer the chillun play with. You carry him a toy hammer and a nail. Well, after you go there and carry him this toy hammer and this nail, you get you a black candle and you carry it to him and you light it there. And I guarantee you it's good.*

(You leave the hammer and nail?)

*You leave the hammer and nail; don't take it away from there.*

(Well, suppose I was living here, where would I find St.

Expedite?)

*You'll find Expedite saint in the church or else in a bookstore—in the book store.*

(Well, you have to bring the saint home, then?)

*Yeah, you bring that saint home and you fix it at your house. But always nail it right at the door where they got to come in.*

(You mean inside the door or above the door?)

*Inside the door—inside the house. And burn that candle and some tape lights [tapers]—always burn the tape lights around it—little red tape lights—well, burn 'em. Expedite Saint is on a horse with swords in his hand and a whole lot of snakes around him. That's the Expedite Saint.* (New Orleans, La., [797], Vol. 1. pp. 863-864).

The above informant actually seems to be describing the iconography of St George where he is typically depicted riding a horse, sword in hand and slaying a dragon (see image next page).

This next interview is somewhat disturbing in that it involves the sacrifice of a chicken in a rather cruel way. I include it for a couple of reasons. One, it would not be a balanced presentation of St. Expedite in the Hyatt texts if it were to be excluded simply because it is disturbing, and secondly, it is reminiscent of a Voudou ritual, although the informant leaves out the various invocations made to St. Expedite and Baron Samedi. Whether or not it is left out by design or because that part of the ritual was lost is impossible to say.

(What do you know about St. Expedite?)

*Well, St. Expedite, he conquers his enemies.*

Woodcut frontispiece of Alexander Barclay, Lyfe of Seynt George (Westminster, 1515). Public domain.

(Well, how would you do that? What would you do with that?)

*Well, if you ever done me a mean, ugly trick and I wants to get rid of you, I wants to give you trouble for doing me something bad, mean well, I'll take a chicken and I'll kill a chicken and I'll gut it and I'll take your name. I'll take your name and put it on a piece of paper in this chicken, after it is picked and cleaned—put your name on a piece of paper in there and then you can take a little sand, a little grave-yard dirt. If there is anybody that you can send to them that would slip into your yard and pick up some of your hair— well, they bring the slip [of hair] to you and you put that in there. Anything concerning you, you use—a dirty handker-chief or anything—you slip that in the chicken. After you get all you can get concerning that person, you slip it into this chicken and you sew the chicken up and you put it in there. And you put your candle and burn the candle plumb till it is used—that for the party who done you something.*

(Now, wait. You fixed that chicken up—what do you do with that chicken now—burn that chicken?)

*The chicken—well, in your house, you see, you got a little room—you put it right there on the floor and you put your candles right there. See, like that. And you just put the chicken there on a little box or something—put it on a stand—just keep the candles burning until they burn out.*

(Use one or any number you want?)

*Yeah, any many.*

(Any color you want?)

*Any color and as many candles as you want because it will conquer all your enemies.*

(I see. Any color chicken will do?)

*Er—ah—is mostly a black chicken.*

(Mostly a black chicken.)

*Is preferred better—a black one, yeah.*

(Why is that?)

*It's just the rule—anything black is evil.* (Mint Owens, 1938, New Orleans, La. Vol. 2 pp. 1087-1088).

********

This concludes the section on the Hyatt texts. Next, we move on to some practical conjures for the practicing rootworker that range from simple to perform to relatively advanced due to the amount of commitment required, as well as some of the ingredients used.

S. SPEDITO MARTIRE

Saint Expeditus, in an oil painting of scenes from his life and martyrdom, n.d. Credit: Wellcome Library, London. Wellcome Images available under Creative Commons Attribution only licence CC BY 4.0.

# CHAPTER 4:
# PRACTICAL CONJURES

## The Lollygag Conjure

For a magickal antidote to lollygagging, dilldallying and just plain putting things off, I offer to you this conjure inspired by my own tendency to engage in the evil deed so aptly described by Frank Hangler of the Oxford Internet Institute (2014):

> Thomas de Quincey claimed it was worse than murder. Krishna declared it a sign of a degenerate soul. For Abraham Lincoln's wife it was her 'evil genius'. Estimates suggest that 80-95% of college students engage in it, and 20% of people are chronic sufferers. Even the Ancient Egyptians bitched about it in hieroglyphics. (Hangler, 2014).

What is "it"? Why procrastination, of course! And it just so happens to be one of St. Expedite's areas of expertise. Which is awesome, since it clearly isn't one of ours. Okay, so if that statement doesn't apply to you, then move on, because the rest if us need to talk...to St. Expedite, that is.

See, the cool thing is that even if we procrastinate, St. Expedite doesn't. So we can lollygag and dillydally all we want; but, if we are careful to ask him to take care of certain issues for us, then he will—as long as we do so in a sincere and effective manner.

The image on the next page is the frontispiece of Anthony Walker's *The Great Evil of Procrastination* (1682) and will serve as the petition paper for this work. Make a copy of it and print it out. You will also need a red candle and St. Expe-

*Jb* THE *Hay 34*

# Great Evil

OF

# PROCRASTINATION.

O R,

The Sinfulness and Danger of
Defering Repentance.

In Several

# DISCOURSES.

By *Anthony Walker*, D. D. Rector
of *Fyfield* in *Essex*.

*LONDON,*

Printed for *Nathanael Ranew* at
the *Kings Arms* in S. *Paul's*
Church-Yard. 1682.

dite oil for this work for expediency.

Set up your altar according to instructions on page 47. Fix a red candle by writing the word "PROCRASTINATION" on the candle with a pin or a nail. Anoint with St. Expedite Oil. Write on the back of the petition paper "PROCRASTINATION" in red ink nine times and turn the paper once to the right and write over and across the words "HODIE" nine times. Set the petition paper under the red candle face down. Light the candle. Say the following prayer nine times in a row and allow the candle to burn down. Once it has burned down completely, burn the petition and scatter it to the four winds. Remember to thank St. Expedite publicly after he grants your request.

## Prayer to Saint Expedite to End Procrastination
*St. Expedite, witness of Faith to the point of martyrdom,*
*in exercise of Good, you make tomorrow today.*
*You live in the fast time of the last minute,*
*always projecting yourself toward the future.*
*Give strength to the heart of the man who doesn't*
*look back and who doesn't postpone.*
*Amen.**

\*\*\*\*\*\*\*\*

*Prayer to end Procrastination is from https://saintexpedite.org/prayers.html

# St. Expedite Dollars

St. Expedite dollars are excellent for drawing money and financial stability. They are also good for helping you pay bills on time and stop procrastinating where that is concerned. Here are a few suggestions for working with St. Expedite dollars.

- To never be without money, always keep a St. Expedite dollar in your wallet or wherever you keep your money.
- Anoint a St. Expedite dollar and place at the bottom of your drawer along with some change to insure money stays with you. Add at least one coin each day you have money.
- Print out one of the dollar bills and anoint it in a five spot pattern with St. Expedite Oil. Five spotting is anointing each of the four corners as well as the middle of the petition paper. On the back of the dollar, write your petition to St. Expedite. Of course, it should be something related to money. Then, place the petition with St. Expedite's face up underneath a candle that is half green and half red. Anoint the green candle and sprinkle a little bit of powdered cinnamon and basil on the candle. Pray the following prayer three times:

*"I ask you, Saint Expedite, to aid me in my financial difficulties. Let your strength support and protect my income and help me to obtain enough money so that I will not suffer need and want. Please let peace and enjoyment reign in my household. I ask you and pray that my wishes be granted, and glorify your intercession. Amen."*

Wrap the wax remains of the candle in the dollar bill and tie closed with string or twine. Place in a green mojo bag and carry it with you for financial luck. Remember to thank him publicly after he grants your request.

# St. Expedite Bottle Spell

This is a bottle spell you can prepare and keep on St. Expedite's altar and work it daily. It is not designed to be disposed of. For this spell you will need the following ingredients:

- Bottle or jar
- Red candle
- Images of St. Expedite, crows, crosses, Virgin of Guadalupe, the planet mercury
- Statue of St. Expedite or framed image
- Red paint
- St. Expedite or Fast Luck Oil
- Metal Cross
- Glass of water
- Sara Lee Pound cake
- Fresh flowers
- Cinnamon stick
- A piece of pyrite
- Magnetic sand
- Feather from a crow, raven or black bird
- White rum
- Herbs: palm, basil, Grains of Paradise seeds, pine, basil, geranium, lilac
- Red stone

You will set up your altar in a triangle formation with the Statue or framed image of St. Expedite on the front right, the glass of water on the front left, and the St. Expedite bottle spell in the back center.

Wash the bottle with salt water and consecrate it to the purpose at hand. Paint the bottle or jar red and affix the image of St. Expedite to the bottle. Add the other images onto the bottle in a manner that pleases you. Write the word "HODIE" on the bottle, or print it out and glue it to the bottle. Attach the cross to a chain or cord and tie around the mouth

of the jar, allowing the cross to hang down in front of St. Expedite's image.

Prepare your candle by washing it with Florida water. Florida water is used to draw things to you. Set it aside to air dry. Anoint with St. Expedite Oil (formula on page 99). Write your petition on a piece of parchment paper with Dove's Blood ink. You can create Dove's Blood ink by adding essence of rose to red ink. Alternately, write your petition with red ink and spray some floral perfume on the paper after you write the petition and anoint with St. Expedite oil.

Place your petition inside the bottle. Add some fresh flower petals, cinnamon stick, piece of pyrite, 7 herbs, magnetic sand, red stone, & crow feather. Top off with the white rum. Stick the red candle into the mouth of the bottle.

Set the bottle on a fire proof dish. Light the candle and pray to St. Expedite:

*Our dear martyr and protector, Saint Expedite,*
*You who know what is necessary and what is urgently needed.*
*I beg you to intercede before the Holy Trinity, that by your*
*grace my request will be granted.*
*(State your petition exactly as it reads in the bottle)*
*May I receive your blessings and favors.*
*In the name of our Lord Jesus Christ, Amen.\**

This is to be said daily until the candle burns all the way down. Keep the bottle on your altar. Continue to pray to St. Expedite daily until he answers your prayer. Then be sure to pay him with a piece of pound cake, fresh flowers, and tell the world how he has helped you.

********

*Prayer from https://saintexpedite.org/prayers.html

# To Fix a St. Expedite Statue

When you first procure a statue of St. Expedite, you will want to cleanse it and fix it for maximum ritual efficacy. To fix a statue is to ritually prepare it for magickal workings.

To begin, rinse off your new statue with a blend of Holy water and rain water. Then anoint it with olive oil, going from top to bottom then bottom to top spreading the oil lightly over all of the statue. While you are doing so, you should be praying to St. Expedite, telling him how you are fixing his statue as a special show of your devotion to him. You can wipe off any excess with a clean white linen cloth.

Some statues and figurines are hallow and when turned upside down there is a visible opening. The inside can be filled with herbs, powders, roots and curios and then sealed with clay or wax. If your statue does not have an opening, you can still fix it by mixing some clay or wax with herbs powders, oils and then spreading it over the base of the statue. If you use polymer clay, you will have to cook it in the oven on a very low temperature—about 175 degrees. This should only be done with ceramic statues. You can mix any herbs that contain the properties that coincide with the needs for which you will be invoking St. Expedite. However, it should contain palm ashes, cinnamon powder, cascarilla, basil, myrrh oil, Grains of Paradise seeds and magnetic sand. If you plan to work with him as a two headed saint, add the ashes of a burned crow feather and powdered human bone. The wax or clay should be spread evenly across the bottom of the statue so that it will stand nicely. Once you have finished preparing the clay, make the sign of the cross(roads) over the statue and leave it on your altar.

********

# To Make a Person Go Away

This work is designed to get rid of a person by energizing the sorcery associated with St. Expedite. Take a black wax melt and knead the wax like dough. You may have to warm it slightly so it is pliable. Write the person's name on a piece of brown paper four times backward and five times forward. Burn the paper and add the ashes to the wax. Then, stick nine small black feathers into the ball. Take the ball to the nearest cemetery and leave it at the base of the largest cross headstone there. Snap your fingers and say "Baron Samedi, see that St. Expedite makes (name of target) go quick." Leave a small bottle of rum along with fifteen cents and Jack of Spades playing card as offerings.

D ALVARADO 20

# Shoe Dressing to Stomp Out Procrastination

Set up St. Expedite's image on your altar and knock three times. Call his name out three times while doing so. Say,

*Through the power of the Holy Trinity, I want you, St. Expedite, to help me stomp out my tendency to put things off tomorrow what should be done today, with every step I take.*

Tell St. Expedite you are sending God after him to be sure he does this favor for you. Write the word "cras" (Latin for "tomorrow") on the bottom of your shoe. Sprinkle the powder in your shoes every day before putting them on. Repeat for nine days and your habit should be broken and your temporal awareness will be much improved.

**Formula for Anti-Procrastination Powder**

- Cornstarch
- Powdered lemon peel
- Palm ash
- Ashes of a burned crow feather

# For Quick Help

This is a very common work known by most rootworkers, though I first posted in on the internet quite a few years ago before his devotion became as popular as it is today among the online conjure demographic. This is how it works.

Light a red candle that has been anointed with St. Expedite oil or Fast Luck Oil and set it next to a glass of water for the Saint. Recite the prayer below daily until the request is granted, then be sure to give Saint Expedite a gift. Allow the candle to burn down. Pray to Saint Expedite:

*Saint Expedite, you who quickly brings things to pass,*
*I come to you and ask that this wish be granted.*
*_____ (Clearly express what you want)*
*Expedite now what I want of you, this very second.*
*Don't waste another day.*
*Grant me what I ask for.*
*Quickly!*
*I know your power, I know you because of your work.*
*I know you can help me.*
*Do this for me and I will spread your name with love and honor so that it will be invoked again and again. Expedite my wish with speed, love, honor, and goodness. Glory to you, Saint Expedite!*

When your request is granted, place fresh cut flowers in the glass of water. Thank St. Expedite by offering him a piece of Sara Lee pound cake and be sure to tell someone how he has helped you. Also place an ad in the newspaper or post on a public forum thanking him, so that his name and glory will grow. If you do not thank him in this manner, it is said he will take back your request and then some, so be sure to remember this step.

********

# To Make a Wish

This is a working described by a New Orleans informant in Volume 1 of the Hyatt texts. To ask for "St. Espidy's" help, set a green candle on his altar. Rap on the altar three times and say a prayer to him and burn the candle at 6:00 to 9:00 in the morning. Listen for him to rap back. Relight the candle at 6:00 in the evening and allow to burn until 9:00 that evening, at which point you are to extinguish the candle. Each time you relight the candle, rap on the altar three times and listen for him to rap back. Repeat this candle burning pattern for nine days, and you will get your wish if you hear him rap back even once. [New Orleans, La. (1558), Vol. 1., 2834:6].

Here is a suggested prayer you may say or tweak to suit your needs:

*I come before you St. Expedite to remedy a special problem in my life (state your problem). I ask for you divine intercession and powerful support to grant me this wish: (state your wish—be specific and realistic). If you grant me this wish, I will give you (tell him what you will give him) and spread your good name. Glory to you, St. Expedite!*

Remember to fulfil any promises you made to him immediately and thank him publicly after he grants your request.

\*\*\*\*\*\*\*\*

# For Help with Money Problems

To ask for St. Expedite's help to protect your money and for help to solve money problems, take a green offertory candle and inscribe on the candle "Protect Money" on one side going in the direction of the candle tip and on the other side inscribe "Remove Debt" going down the candle towards the bottom. You may inscribe different words to better suit your specific needs. Anoint the candle with St. Expedite oil. Set the candle at the top of the triangle altar formation, say the prayer below and allow the candle to burn down.

*Saint Expedite, I come to you and humbly ask for your*
*assistance with (clearly state your need)*
*Please do this for me in a hurry. Grant me what I ask for now.*
*I know your power, I know you can help me.*
*Do this for me and I will spread your name with love and honor*
*so that it will be invoked again and again. Expedite this wish*
*with speed, love, honor, and goodness.*
*Glory to you, Saint Expedite!*

Remember to fulfill any promises you make to him immediately and thank him publicly after he grants your request.

********

### Conjure Tip

Take a dollar bill and attach a St. Expedite dollar to the face of the bill. Anoint the four corners of the bill and the center with St. Expedite oil. Write a petition on the edge of the bill. For example, "Bless me with abundance in money and free me from debt. Protect and guard my money, home and family. Glory be to you St Expedite!" Laminate the dollar bill or frame it and hang it above the front door of your home.

# For Success and Prosperity

This is a simple and quick way to petition St. Expedite for success and proserity. Burn a green votive candle to St. Expedite on Monday, Wednesday and Friday—three different candles, each day.

*Be Quick, St. Expedite!*
*Grant my wish before your candle burns out,*
*And I will magnify your name.*
*(State your petition)*
*Amen.*

On the third day after the candle burns down, take the wax remains from each day, place in a paper bag and bury in your front yard if your petition was to draw something to you. If it was to take something away, then toss it in the trash outside.

\*\*\*\*\*\*\*\*\*

## The Society of St. Expeditus in the Philippines

For over 22 years, the Society of St. Expeditus has been promoting the devotion to this advocate of urgent cases. Besides help in financial problems and physical illness, St. Expeditus is believed to have interceded for United States visa applicants. The image of St. Expeditus was enthroned for the first time at St. Andrew Church in La Huerta, Parañaque, on April 10, 1994 when Fr. Omer Prieto was parish priest. the Society of St. Expeditus revived the devotion to St. Expeditus, advocate of urgent cases, in fulfillment of a promise made by the Buencamino sisters: Milagros Gonzalez, Nanette Sinco, Nida Lopez, Aro Pardo and their brothers. Since the revival of the cult of devotion, the number of devotees has been increasing by leaps and bounds (Source: The Philippines Daily Inquirer, 2008 and 2009).

# Lucky Lottery

Here's a work for folks who like to gamble and play the lottery. This is a three day work, but is not done three days in a row; rather, it is done Monday, Wednesday and Friday, each day burning a separate, different color candle, for a different purpose towards the ultimate goal of increasing luck in games of chance.

On a Monday, burn a white votive candle to open roads. On a Wednesday, burn a red candle to speed the work up and give it a Mercurial power boost. On Friday, burn a green candle to cinch the deal with money and luck. Each day, say the following prayer to St. Expedite. Be sure to fulfill your vow as soon as he grants your petition. Do not even wait a day.

*Saint Expedite,*
*You who quickly brings things to pass,*
*I come to you in need —*

*(state your petition)*

*Do this for me St. Expedite,*
*And when it is accomplished,*
*I will as rapidly reply for my part*
*With an offering to you.*

*(State your vow or promise)*

*Be Quick, St. Expedite!*
*Grant my wish before your candle burns out,*
*And I will magnify your name.*
*Amen.*

\*\*\*\*\*\*\*\*

# Flying Novena to Get a Partner

A flying novena is a novena said for an emergency. Novenas are typically said over a period of nine days. A flying novena is said every hour for nine hours. Unlike the Nine Hour or Nine Day Novena, the flying novena is the only prayer said nine times, nine hours in a row. It differs from the Nine Hour Novena in that it is a single prayer said as opposed to a collection of prayers.

Take a silver dime and wrap it in a piece of red cloth with a pinch of palm ash and a rose petal onto which you have written the name of the one with whom you wish to be. On another rose petal, write your name. Place the rose petals face to face. Anoint with rose oil and tie closed. Then, place the paket on St. Expedite's altar and light a red candle and say the following flying novena.

## The Flying Novena

*O St. Expedite, you who brings things to pass Most expeditiously, remind me of the words of Jesus who has said, "Ask and you shall receive, seek and you shall find, knock and it shall be opened to you." Through the intercession of Mary, Your Most Holy Mother, I knock, I seek, and I ask that my prayer be granted as quickly as possible. (State your request)*

After saying the flying novena nine times, nine hours in a row, carry the paket with you to have the blessings of St. Expedite with you always. Then when you need him, hold the paket and snap your fingers and request his assistance. Be sure to publicly thank him when he helps you.

*********

# Spiced Bullet Talisman

This is a work that calls for fixing a bullet with hot and spicy ingredients which is prayed over and then left on St. Expedite's altar for nine days to charge it up. It is then worn on a necklace or placed in a charm bag to imbue anything it touches with the power of expediency. For this work you will need:

- Empty bullet casing
- Red cinnamon wax melt
- Cinnamon chips
- Nutmeg shavings
- Allspice berry
- Fire ant dirt
- Cayenne pepper
- Ghost chili
- Honey granules
- Rose petals if for love, piece of pyrite of for money, burned copy of court papers for legal issues
- Slip of paper with the word "Hodie" written on it
- Red candle

First, take the utmost care with preparing this talisman as any number of the ingredients can burn your skin upon contact and you don't want to know what can happen to your eyes should you inadvertently wipe them before washing your hands first For this reason, it is recommended you use surgical gloves when preparing the talisman, and be sure to wash your hands thoroughly with hot soapy water after you are finished sealing it with the wax.

Set up your altar to St. Expedite and light a red candle. Knock on the altar three times or ring the bell three times while calling out his name three times.

You only need a very small amount of each of the above ingredients to fill a bullet casing. Begin with placing the ingredient that represents the primary purpose of the talis-

Bullet casing and wax melts

man: rose petal if for love, piece of pyrite if for money, or a pinch of burned court papers if for legal issues. Say the following prayer when doing so:

*Glorious St. Expedite.*
*You who know the needs that challenge us,*
*I beg you to intercede before the Holy Trinity and grant me the grace of (state your intention).*

Take the slip of paper and write the word "Hodie" in red ink on it. Fold it towards you three times. Place on top of the primary ingredient and say the following:

*St. Expedite, come to my assistance;*
*Make haste to help me, today with (state your intention).*

Take a pinch of each of cinnamon chips, nutmeg shavings,

allspice berry, fire ant dirt, cayenne pepper, ghost chili flakes and honey granules and load into the bullet casing, leaving about 1/8 to 1/4 space from the end of the casing. With each ingredient, say the following prayer:

*Glorious St. Expedite,*
*I beg you to intercede before the Holy Trinity and grant me the grace of (state your petition).*

Take the cinnamon wax melt and push it into the end of the bullet casing and remove the excess wax. Heat the end of the wax allowing it to melt into the bullet. Add more wax to thoroughly seal the ingredients inside. Leave the bullet casing on St. Expedite's altar in front of the candle for nine days. Light a new candle each day, so you can use tea lights, tapers or votives. Each day, say the following prayer:

*My Saint Expedite of urgent and just causes,*
*please intercede for me with power of the Holy Trinity.*
*Bless this talisman for me,*
*You who are a Holy warrior and Saint of expediency,*
*Imbue this talisman with (Clearly express what you want, and ask him to find a way to get it to you.)*
*My Saint Expedite,*
*Make this talisman Most powerful and*
*respond to my plea with urgency.*
*I will be grateful to you for the rest of my life*
*and I will offer you pound cake and spread your good name publicly so all will rejoice in your glory and good deeds.*
*Amen.*
*(Say one Our Father, one Hail Mary, and make the sign of the cross.)*

On the ninth day and after the last candle has burned down, take the talisman and keep it in a red mojo bag. Carry it with you to have the blessings of St. Expedite with you wherever you go.

# Protection Ward

This is an adaptation of an old New Orleans work documented in 1946 by Robert Tallant (see page 38). For a protective ward for your home, take a silver dime and wash it with salt water and rinse with Florida water. Then, cut out a small image of St. Expedite and glue it to the dime. Place the dime on top of the front door sill for protection.

Another way to use this dime is to glue it to a railroad spike and drive the spike into the ground by your front door. If you don't have yard or garden into which to drive it , put it into a potted palm tree by your front door.

**\*\*\*\*\*\*\*\***

# Wax Wishing Balls

This work is one you will do over a period of three days and consists of three colors of wax an different herbs. The work is to be done on Monday, Wednesday and Friday. For this work you will need:

- White wax
- Yellow wax
- Green wax
- Camphor
- Eucalyptus
- Master Root
- Alfalfa
- Five Finger grass
- Gold magnetic sand
- Gold lodestones or pieces of pyrite (will be the center of each wax ball made)

On Monday, melt the white wax and add the camphor and eucalyptus to the wax. As it cools form it into little balls around a gold lodestone. Stick a toothpick into each of the balls. Place them on a white dish on St. Expedite's altar and say the following prayer:

*Saint Expedite,*
*You who quickly brings things to pass,*
*I ask that you empower this wax with*
*Your expediency to make my wishes happen*
*In a hurry. Do this for me St. Expedite,*
*And when it is accomplished,*
*I will as rapidly magnify your name.*
*Amen.*

On Wednesday, melt the yellow wax and add master root and alfalfa. As the wax cools, dip the white balls of wax into the yellow wax and cover well. Place them back on the white dish on St. Expedite's altar and say the following prayer:

*Saint Expedite,*
*You who quickly brings things to pass,*
*I ask that you empower this wax with*
*Your expediency to make my wishes happen*
*In a hurry. Do this for me St. Expedite,*
*And when it is accomplished,*
*I will as rapidly magnify your name.*
*Amen.*

On Friday, melt the green wax and add five finger grass and gold magnetic sand. As the wax cools, dip the yellow wax balls into the green wax until completely covered. Remove the toothpicks and smooth over the hole with the green wax. Place them back on the white dish on St. Expedite's altar and say the following prayer:

*Saint Expedite,*
*You who quickly brings things to pass,*
*I ask that you empower this wax with*
*Your expediency to make my wishes happen*
*In a hurry. Do this for me St. Expedite,*
*And when it is accomplished,*
*I will as rapidly magnify your name.*
*Amen.*

When you have an immediate need, take one of the wax balls to a river or other body of moving water. Make your wish on the wax ball. Snap your fingers three times and say, "St. Expedite! Grant my wish and I will spread the glory of your name! (state your wish). Do it now St. Expedite!" Toss the ball into the river. When he grants your wish, be sure to immediately give him public praise and a piece of pound cake.

********

# Hot Penny Activators to Fire Up your Finances

These are pennies charged and blessed on St. Expedite's altar that will serve to activate your money and stimulate your finances. After they are charged they are to be kept with your change and your regular money. Get a green bowl and fill with Dragon's blood resin, parsley, magnetic sand and cinnamon chips. Take nine shiny copper pennies and cleanse with Hoyt's Cologne, Florida Water or Fast Luck Water (see formula in this section) and add to the bowl. Set St. Expedite's image behind the bowl. Take a pinch of the parsley, Dragon's Blood and magnetic sand and powder it in a mortar and pestle. Cleanse a green candle with Florida water, allow to air dry and anoint with St. Expedite oil. Then, roll in the powdered herbs. Get St. Expedite's attention by ringing a bell and calling out his name three times or by knocking on the altar three times in front of the bowl. Light the fixed green candle in front of the bowl. Tell St. Expedite: "By the Power of the Holy Trinity, I ask you to do this favor for me. Give these pennies the power to increase my money three fold whenever they touch my wallet, purse, bank statements, coins, and dollar bills. In return, I promise to spread your good name as an excellent servant of God. Expedite this wish with speed, love, honor, and goodness. Glory to you, Saint Expedite!" Remember to fulfil any promises you made to him immediately and thank him publicly after he grants your request

# Signifying Salt

An informant from Algiers in the Hyatt texts when discussing St. Expedite describes briefly the use of red rock salt as a signifier for harm. "A piece of red rock salt" the informant reports, placed "behin' de front do'" will sweat when anyone enters who intends to harm you (Vol. 3 p. 1904). Using this information, one could keep a chunk of red rock salt or salt lamp on St. Expedite's altar to be observed when people enter the home. If it begins to sweat when someone enters, you can politely ask them to leave. Then get to cleansing your space by smudging it with sage, sprinkling it with holy water and anointing doors and windows with St. Expedite oil while praying the prayer of protection from haters.

### Prayer to St. Expedite for Quick Protection from Haters
*St. Expedite, You are the Holy Warrior and*
*Defender of righteousness,*
*Protect me from the evils that lurk around me and*
*keep away those who just want my downfall.*
*Silence the slanderous tongues that wag*
*in the darkness that is their souls.*
*Bind the hands who will lift up against me and my family.*
*Thwart all attempts to sabotage my success and*
*Remove all barriers that are placed in my way.*
*Stomp on the arrogance and grandiosity*
*that feeds the destructive egos of my enemies.*
*Today I ask you to grant me the grace of*
*(state your petition clearly and precisely)*
*and I promise to spread your name and ability*
*to protect and defend the vulnerable*
*and to silence hateful people.*
*Amen.*

# Portable St. Expedite Shrine

This is one of my favorite conjures that uses an Altoid tin. It is very easy to make and you can make several of them at one time prepared for different purposes. This particular one is a money draw shrine with a built in candle. Once you make this one, you will see how easy it can be to make them for a variety of purposes by substituting the wax color, essential oils and herbs to suit your need.

For this work, you will need the following items:

- Candle wick and candle wick metal bases
- Beeswax
- Pliers
- Glue stick
- Alfalfa
- Basil
- Cinnamon essential oil
- Image of St. Expedite
- Three pennies
- Pliers

First, glue St. Expedite's image to the inner lid of the Altoid tin. Glue three pennies in a triangle shape on the image. Then, cut the wick to about an inch taller than the tin. Thread the wick through the metal base the pinch the base closed with the pliers. Glue the metal base to the center of the Altoid tin. Melt the beeswax in a double boiler and once it is completely melted, add the herbs and essential oil. Carefully pour the melted wax into the tin, leaving about a 1/4 to 1/8 inch from the top, taking care the wick does not fall into the bottom. Allow the wax to set for several hours. Close the tin and keep for emergencies or take with you when traveling.

*Note: Be sure to burn on a fire proof surface as the tin will get hot as the wax burns.

# Formula for St. Expedite Oil

- Rose essential oil or fragrance oil
- Carnation essential oil
- Cinnamon essential oil
- Lodestone
- Alkanet root (just a pinch for the red color)

Add the above to a base of mineral oil. Use to anoint self, altar items, St. Expedite; image or statue and petitions papers.

## Formula for St. Expedite Attraction Spray

- Rose water
- Rain water
- Lodestone
- Cinnamon essential oil
- Dried red rose petals
- Everclear or perfumers alcohol

Combine the above ingredients going light on the cinnamon as it will overpower everything if not careful. Add10% alcohol and leave it on St. Expedite's altar. Spray yourself, home and office to draw luck, success, love or money.

********

# Fast Luck Water

This is a fabulous Fast Luck Water you can make to use as the basis of a room spray, add to a spiritual bath, floor wash or hand wash. Using herbs and spices that are traditionally used with St. Expedite, it is placed on the altar and left for the life of a candle and blessed by the Minute Saint upon request

Set up a traditional St. Expedite altar in a triangle formation. Place a green candle at the top, place St. Expedite's image right side up to the right and a bouquet of red flowers to the left. In the center, place a clear glass of fresh rain water into which you have placed a single cinnamon stick, some basil and rosemary. Surround the glass with fresh money herbs like basil, and parsley. Knock on the altar three times while calling out St. Expedite's name. Then, tell him to imbue this water with the power to make things happen fast Leave the water on his altar covered until the candle finishes burning so it doesn't evaporate. Then, proceed to add to floor washes, spiritual baths and hand washes for fast luck.

********

## St. Expedite at St. Alphonsus Church in Wexford, Pennsylvania

Forever and a day has been the rumor that St. Expedite does not exist anywhere in the United States except at Our Lady of Guadalupe chapel. For more than a century, however, St. Alphonsus Church has served the Catholic population of Wexford, Pennsylvania. On October 10, 1937, Father Angel officiated at the formal dedication of three shrines built in the Old World style of native stone. They shelter the terra cotta statues imported from Italy that honor Our Lady of Olives, protectress against lightning; St. Kateri Tekakwitha, the Lily of the Mohawks; and Saint Expedite, patron of emergencies and expeditious solutions. At the time of the shrine dedication, Army planes flew overhead and dropped flowers. Local pilots were invited to take part in the service. Although St. Expedite often is referred to as the patron saint for expeditious solutions, the literature from the unveiling refers to him as the patron saint of aviators and air travelers. The shrine to St. Expedite was donated in memory of Herman P. Brandt. (http://saintalphonsuswexford.org/about-us/our-church-grounds/shrines-statues).

# Magic Lamp To Get a Job

For this work you will need a hurricane lamp. Although magic lamps can be made using any number of receptacles, hurricane lamps have always been plentiful in New Orleans and are perfect for this kind of work. Magic lamps are powerful conjures as they burn hotter than candles and the spirit is called to mount the lamp through attraction to the ingredients and prayer. Fill the lamp with 3/4 olive oil and 1/4 red palm oil. Write the name of the company or position you wish to get on a piece of brown paper nine times. Attach it to the bottom of the wick with a safety pin. Draw St. Expedite's vévé and set the lamp on the vévé (see page 105). Sprinkle some cinnamon, allspice and lemon verbena on top of the oil. Add a few drops of rose oil. Lower the wick to be sure it is saturated with the oil then pull it back up and light the lamp. Roll the wick down to a low flame. Then recite the prayer for a job to St. Expedite:

*Glorious St. Expedite, I call upon your power, speed and ability to come to my assistance and help me to gain employment. Quickly, bring to me (state your need). Grant me my petition with haste, and I will spread the glory of your good name. Amen.*

After saying the prayer, light a rose scented Our Lady of Guadalupe candle and set it before the lamp. This is so that she goes before St. Expedite to smooth the way for him to do his work for you. Every day, relight the lamp, say the prayer, and relight the OLG candle. Whenever the lamp is lit, the candle should be lit. Once the candle burns all the way down the work is done.

# St. Expedite Death Conjure

There are many death conjures in New Orleans Voudou and I have elected not to include a multitude of them here. The reader is welcome to refer to my other books, *The Voodoo Hoodoo Spellbook* (2011) and *The Voodoo Doll Spellbook* (2014) for more information on this type of work. I have chosen to include one such work here with St. Expedite to illustrate his versatility. It is provided for educational purposes only and its inclusion by no means endorses the use of magick to cause the death of a person.

For this work, you need a large black candle. Cut off the top of the candle making it the base and turn the candle over and carve the base into a tip. Inscribe your enemy's name backwards onto the candle with a rusty nail. Dip the candle in thunder water (rain water collected during a thunderstorm). In this way, you are amplifying St. Expedite's warrior aspect as leader of the Thundering Legion. Allow it to air dry.

Set up St. Expedite's altar in an inverted manner, meaning the point of the triangle will be in the front instead of the back. Turn his image upside down. If you have a statue, set him upside down in a dish of black witch's salt, or set him upside down on the floor under the altar.

Light the candle and allow it to burn for three hours. At the end of the three hours, pinch it out by dampening your fingertips with thunder water. When you do so, say, "In the name of the Father, Son and Holy Ghost, with the Barons of the cemetery and the speed of St. Expedite, let my enemy (name) drop dead (get killed in a car crash, be murdered-whatever your devilish flavor)." Leave the candle be for three hours and relight it and repeat. Do this one more time for a total of three times in one day. Then, repeat for two more days: 3 hours burning the candle, 3 hours break, 3 hours burning the candle, three hours break, three hours burning the candle, three hours break. On the last day, take what is left of the candle and wrap it in a piece of black fabric along with some graveyard dirt and the person's name written on a piece of trash. Tie it closed and dip in motor oil and take it to the cemetery and bury it as close to the center of the cemetery as you can get. Pour black pepper over it and some sulphur and light it on fire and say:

*"In the sweat of thy face shalt thou eat bread, till thou return unto the ground; for out of it wast thou taken: for dust thou art, and unto dust shalt thou return."* (Genesis 3:19, KJV).

Be sure everything is covered with earth, and drive that rusted nail you used to carve the candle with into the ground right above the paket. Be sure it is completely in the ground and not sticking up and showing. Then leave the cemetery, being sure to leave fifteen cents and a bottle of rum at the gates in gratitude. Never speak the person's name aloud again, lest you call their soul to you. When your petition has been answered, turn St. Expedite right side up and return his altar to regular formation. Thank him by making a public statement of gratitude, but never speak of the work you have done to anyone. You should also give him white rum and red roses for this one.

Note that should you take it upon yourself to do this work, do not attempt to contact me for assistance or advice. This work is included for it's anthropological value only and is not meant as a tutorial for murder by magick.

**\*\*\*\*\*\*\*\***

# Graveyard Work with St. Expedite

This is a basic ritual for designating a special spot from which you can do graveyard work with St. Expedite. Find the oldest grave in the cemetery with a cross. Ask the spirit of the grave if they would allow you to use this gravesite as the place for working with St. Expedite and Baron Samedi. If it feel right, proceed to draw St. Expedite's sigil (opposite page) with a blend of red brick dust and palm ash on the ground in front of the grave. Place some offerings to St. Expedite and Baron Samedi in a bowl on top of the sigil. Offerings can include Louisiana hot sauce, rum spiced with 21 of the hottest peppers you can get, peanuts, pork rinds, creole seasoning, popcorn, pound cake and black coffee. Place a cross in the bowl. Light one red candle for St. Expedite, one black candle for Baron Samedi, and one white candle for the Holy Trinity. Do this ritual at 12 noon or 12 midnight.

### Prayer to St. Expedite in the Cemetery

*St. Expedite I implore you with the power of the Holy Trinity and guidance of Baron Samedi, Guardian of the Cemetery, I knock on this grave three times, and three times I call out your name. I hereby name you my patron and this our sacred space. I ask that you protect me from those who will commit acts of evil and injustice against me. Retract and revoke all acts of treachery that have been committed against me. Allow me to walk out of this sacred space protected and empowered. This petition is enforced by the order of Baron Samedi. So be it! Amen.*

This ritual only needs to be performed once, unless you change locations or designate a spot in another cemetery. Now when you need something of a serious nature or of a left-handed nature, this will be a good spot to make those petitions. When you are done, pay the Baron with rum and peanuts, leave the cemetery in silence, and leave 9 pennies at the gate as payment. Then be sure to pay St. Expedite in the manner in which you promised.

# For Quick Money, Keep Him with Green

Green herbs and vegetables are often used to surround candles and adorn St. Expedite's altar for money works.

*St Espidee. Well now, dey always used him fo' money. Yo' got to always keep 'im wit green. Yo' burn 'im a green candle evah mawnin' 'fore nine o'clock. Yo' burn a green candle an' yo' g ive' im a glass of rain watah, cistern watah [cistern collects rain water from roof of house]. Gits a purity white glass [an uncolored drinking glass] an' yo' put dat glass intuh a white saucer, an' puts it anywhere dere a pitchure, wheresomevah yo' want 'em wit dat pitcher [of the saint]. An' git chew some green onions—AH KNOW YO' KNOW WHUT GREEN ONIONS IS—an' parsley an' dat green candle, an' ah'll bet chew dat yo' goin' git money an' yo' don' know how yo' got it.*

[In the preceding rite a green candle is put in a clear drinking glass full of rain water. Then glass with candle is set into a white saucer and surrounded by green onions and parsley. All this is placed beneath or in front of a picture of St. Expedite. The candle is lighted.] (Hyatt, Vol. 3, p. 2125)

Note that the "translation" of the spell by Hyatt in the brackets above may not be entirely accurate. He interprets "purity white glass" with "a clear drinking glass" when the informant probably meant a "purty (pretty) white glass" to be set on the saucer. This is but one of many examples of potential mistakes made by Hyatt in the thousands of pages of interviews recorded due to an unfamiliarity with southern Black dialect and culture. Whether the rain water is in a clear glass or a white glass, in the context of folk magic, the outcome would likely be the same, however. It is for the sake of the integrity of our ancestors that I mention the indiscrepancy in the transcription and translation of the words spoken.

# St. Expedite Confessional Wall To Get Rid of Guilt and Regret

This is a blockbuster work, something to be done if you are experiencing severe obstacles that are related to your past behaviors and choices, or to past victimization that has resulted in your feeling badly about yourself. Self-limiting messages feed blockages, and we often stay stuck because we can't get beyond the internal dialogue that gets in the way of progress and self-actualization. So, this ritual gives you a structured way to get these thoughts and feelings out by naming them, writing them down and posting them on a ritual wall or board to be dissipated and transformed so that you can move forward.

To get rid of feelings of guilt and regret with the help of St.

Expedite, you will need to create a blank sacred space or a confessional wall. A portion of a wall is perfect for this ritual. It can be a wall of wood, like a portion of a wooden fence, a frame with chicken wire or an interlaced wall of sticks or bamboo. You could even use a bulletin board. Set this wall up behind your normal altar for St. Expedite. Do not turn him upside down for this confessional wall. Anoint the wall with St. Expedite Oil in a 5 spot pattern (4 corners and center).

Take some palm ashes and draw a cross on the wall. Don't worry if it doesn't show. Use ashes of cedar or sage if you don't have palm. You can also attach a cross to the wall, a palm frond and a prayer card. When you draw the cross, ask St. Expedite to take all that you place on the wall and get rid of it for you. Each day, take a few moments of silent self-reflection and identify something in your innerost Self that you want to get rid of. Write it down and attach it to the wall. At the end of the month, gather all of your guilt and regrets and burn them. Scatter them to the four winds and as you do so, tell St. Expedite to make them go quick. Be sure to thank him when your feelings dissipate. Repeat this monthly until you have made the breakthrough you need to move forward.

********

Traditional St. Expedite Altar Set Up.

# CHAPTER 5:

## The Prayers
### Daily Devotionals, Minute Prayers, Novenas, and Standard Catholic Prayers

Saint Expeditus, in an oil painting of scenes from his life and martyrdom .Credit: Wellcome Library, London. Wellcome Images Copyrighted work available under Creative Commons Attribution only license CC BY 4.0.

# Prayer to Glorious St. Expedite

The following prayer is found at the foot of the statue of the saint in the city of Santa Fe, Argentina.

*Glorious St. Expedite! Great have been*
*the merits of your unwavering faith in us*
*turns your virtues and have been imitating you,*
*prefer the heavenly delights of worldly temptations.*
*Be our guide and help us navigate our earthly life with hope.*
*We pray fervently relief for those who suffer and*
*your intercession with Jesus, our Saviour,*
*to open the gates of heaven*
*that await the souls in purgatory.*
*Through Jesus ChriSt our Lord.*

This is a great prayer to say as a daily devotional. Light white candle to St. Expedite for a general devotional. When he answers your petition, make an immediate public statement of gratitude.

SAINT

# A Nine Hour Novena to
# St. Expedite

Set up St. Expedite's altar as shown on pages 47 and 109. Once his altar is set up and you are ready to petition him, turn his image upside down. This signifies a work is in progress. Then, ring the bell three times while calling out his name. This is to wake him up and get his attention. If you do not have a silver bell, tap on the glass of water with a fork or spoon three times while calling his name. Then proceed with the novena, reciting the set of prayers on the hour every hour for 9 hours. Once you start, you must commit to nine hours of devotion. Note that the practice of turning the image of a saint upside down comes from New Orleans Voudou and is not a Catholic tradition. Some folks will place the image upside down under the altar itself.

Upon completion of the novena, be prepared to offer him public thanks and recommend his invocation to others by commenting on any other public forum or advertising section of a newspaper. You may also give him a piece of pound cake and some red flowers if you wish.

In Catholicism, a novena is a traditional nine day prayer that is said at the same time nine days in a row. Novenas are usually said when petitioning a saint for something, but they can also be said as prayers of thanksgiving. The Nine Hour Novena to St. Expedite is performed for nine hours in a row as opposed to nine days in a row and consists of six Catholic prayers each hour. It begins with the *Act of Contrition* prayer and then each hour a special prayer is said for a specific reason followed by a specific number of *Our Fathers, Memorare,* and *Hail Marys.* The individual prayers address faith, hope, freedom, strength, detachment, freedom from anger, grace to pray well, purity and perseverance. The concluding prayer to St. Expedite is said at the end of the 9th hour when all prayers have been said. The standard Catholic prayers are provided on page 134 for those who do not know them.

Note that the Nine Hour Novena to St. Expedite is effective as a road opener novena, so if you are experiencing a significant amount of emotional, situational or conditional blockages in your life, this novena should be very effective if performed correctly.

The Nine Hour Novena is to be said in the following order:
1. Act of Contrition (to be said when beginning)
2. Fifty Four Prayers to Saint Expedite in total (not counting the act of Contrition or Closing Prayer), six per hour for nine hours straight plus additional prayers as indicated, followed by the sign of the cross.
3. Concluding Prayer (after all hourly prayers are said), followed by the sign of the cross.

## Making the Sign of the Cross (roads)

For those unfamiliar with making the sign of the cross, it is an act of blessing oneself through tracing a cross (roads) shape on the body while saying what is called the trinitarian formula: "In the name of the Father, and the Son, and the Holy Spirit, Amen." The formula may be said aloud or to oneself. The sign of the cross is a ritual motion performed using the right hand and using three fingers representing the Holy Trinity (including the thumb). Specific areas of the body may be touched or just symbolically touched. Begin by touching the forehead while saying "In the name of the Father" (*In nomine Patris* in Latin), then the heart area while saying "And the Son" (*et Filii*) then touching across the shoulders left to right saying "And the Holy Spirit" (*et Spiritus Sanctus*), ending with "Amen."

Pope Innocent III (1198-1216) stated we "make the sign of the cross from the left to the right, because from misery (left) we must cross over to glory (right), just as Christ crossed over from death to life, and from Hades to Paradise."

## Act of Contrition

*My LORD Jesus Christ, Father of endless charity, I am heartily sorry for my sins. Grant me, therefore, pardon of my sins and the grace I ask of You through the merits of the sorrows of Your loving Mother and the virtues of Your martyr, Saint Expedite.*

## FIRST HOUR

On the first hour of the novena, it is recommended to pray for the gift of faith.

*O Glorious Martyr, Saint Expedite, through the lively faith which was granted you by Bon Dieu (God), I ask you to awaken the same faith in my heart, that I may also believe wholeheartedly that there is a Good God, but most importantly that I may be saved from offending Him.*

Follow with:
1. Three Our Fathers in honor of the Most Holy Trinity.
2. One Memorare to the Blessed Virgin Mary.
3. One Hail Mary in Honor of Our Lady of Sorrows.

## SECOND HOUR

On the second hour of the Novena, we pray for the gift of hope for ourselves and for those who have trouble believing.

*O Glorious Martyr, Saint Expedite, through the admirable hope given you by Bon Dieu (God), I pray that those of little belief may be penetrated by some rays of hope so that they also receive eternal blessings; please pray that ardent hope in Bon Dieu be also given me and hold me steadfast in the midst of sufferings.*

Follow with:
1. Three Our Fathers in honor of the Most Holy Trinity.
2. One Memorare to the Blessed Virgin Mary.
3. One Hail Mary in Honor of Our Lady of Sorrows.

## THIRD HOUR

On the third hour of the Novena to Saint Expedite, we pray for freedom from worldly cares, so that we can love Bon Dieu (God) more fully.

*O Glorious Martyr, Saint Expedite, through the endless love which Our Lord planted in your heart, please remove from mine all the shackles tied by worldliness, that without them I may love only Bon Dieu (God) in all eternity. Amen.* (Note the prayer specifically addresses the removal of obstacles.)

Follow with:
1. Three Our Fathers in honor of the Most Holy Trinity.
2. One Memorare to the Blessed Virgin Mary.
3. One Hail Mary in Honor of Our Lady of Sorrows.

## FOURTH HOUR

On the fourth hour of the Novena to Saint Expedite, we pray for the strength to carry the cross of our passions.

*O Glorious Martyr, Saint Expedite, who knew fully well the teaching of the Divine Teacher to carry the cross and follow Him, ask Him for the graces I need that I may fight my own passions.*

Follow with:
1. Three Our Fathers in honor of the Most Holy Trinity.
2. One Memorare to the Blessed Virgin Mary.
3. One Hail Mary in Honor of Our Lady of Sorrows.

## FIFTH HOUR

On the fifth hour of the Novena to Saint Expedite, we pray for the grace of detachment (an oddly Buddhist concept but very worthwhile nonetheless).

*O Glorious Martyr, Saint Expedite, through the bountiful graces you received from Heaven that you may conserve all your vir-*

tues, grant also that I may get rid of all the feelings that block my way to Heaven. (Note this is a road opening prayer)

Follow with:
1. Three Our Fathers in honor of the Most Holy Trinity.
2. Memorare to the Blessed Virgin Mary.
3. One Hail Mary in Honor of Our Lady of Sorrows.

## SIXTH HOUR

On the sixth hour of the Novena to Saint Expedite, we pray for freedom from anger.

*O Glorious Martyr, Saint Expedite, through the sufferings and humiliations which you received for the love of Bon Dieu (God), grant me also this grace which is very pleasing to Bon Dieu, and free me from anger and hardness of heart which is the stumbling block of my soul.* (Note this is a road opening prayer through the invocation for the removal of emotional obstacles)

Follow with:
1. Three Our Fathers in honor of the Most Holy Trinity.
2. One Memorare to the Blessed Virgin Mary.
3. One Hail Mary in Honor of Our Lady of Sorrows.

## SEVENTH HOUR

On the seventh hour of the Novena to Saint Expedite, we pray for the grace to pray well.

*O Glorious Martyr, Saint Expedite, you know that prayer is the golden key that will open the Kingdom of Heaven, teach me to pray in a manner which is desirable to Our Lord and to His Heart, that I may live only for Him, that I may die only for Him, and that I may pray only to Him in all eternity.*

Follow with:
1. Three Our Fathers in honor of the Most Holy Trinity.

2. One Memorare to the Blessed Virgin Mary.
3. One Hail Mary in Honor of Our Lady of Sorrows.

## EIGHTH HOUR

On the eighth hour of the Novena to Saint Expedite, we pray for purity of heart.

*O Glorious Martyr, Saint Expedite, through the clean desire that reigned in all your feelings, word and actions, please let them guide me also in my endless search for the glory of Bon Dieu (God) and the good of my fellowmen.* (Note this is a cleansing prayer)

Follow with:
1. Three Our Fathers in honor of the Most Holy Trinity.
2. One Memorare to the Blessed Virgin Mary.
3. One Hail Mary in Honor of Our Lady of Sorrows.

## NINTH HOUR

On the ninth hour of the Novena to Saint Expedite, we pray for the grace of final perseverance.

*O Glorious Martyr, Saint Expedite, who was so much loved by the Queen of Heaven, that to you nothing was denied, ask her, please my advocate, that through the sufferings of her Divine Son and her own sorrows, I may receive this day the grace I ask of you; but above all the grace to die first before I commit any mortal sin. Amen.* (Note this is a prayer that appeals to St. Expedite to specifically petition Mother Mary in the form of Our Lady of Sorrows on our behalf.)

Follow with:
1. Three Our Fathers in honor of the Most Holy Trinity.
2. One Memorare to the Blessed Virgin Mary.
3. One Hail Mary in Honor of Our Lady of Sorrows.

## Concluding Prayer (after all hourly prayers are said)

*Oh Saint Expedite, my protector, in you I place my hope that my petitions may be granted if they are for my own good. Please ask Our Lord, through the intercession of the Blessed Virgin, for the forgiveness of my sins, and the grace to change my life, particularly the grace ... (state here your petition or grace desired) and I promise to follow your examples and I will recommend your devotion to others.*

Take note of the caveat "if they are for my own good" in this final prayer. This tells us that the Nine Hour Novena to St. Expedite is to be used for positive purposes - blessing, healings, getting a job or getting out of debt for example - as opposed to nefarious reasons like harming an enemy or coercing a person to love you. For these latter purposes, one should appeal to St. Expedite with Baron Samedi and not through a novena or other more traditional Catholic means.

## Final Instructions

When you are done with your prayers, allow the candle to burn down. Leave his altar set up until your petition is answered. Often results are seen before this novena is even completed. If this happens, be sure to complete the novena anyway. Turn his image right side up when your prayer is answered and publicly thank him in. Throw any ritual remains at a crossroads or in the trash.

# Triduum in Honor of St. Expedite to Obtain a Special Favor

A Triduum is a three day religious observance where a set of prayers are said each day, similar to a novena. When you have an urgent request, read the Triduum to St. Expedite and your petition will be granted quickly. Use a white candle for the Triduum and offer him red flowers and a public statement of gratitude after he grants your request.

### First day

*Preface: Oh most merciful Lord, I humbly prostrate myself before Thy Infinite Majesty, and dedicate to Thy glory the devout prayers which I now present to Thee, as an act of devotion to your servant, St Expedite, whose intercession I am now imploring.*

*Most honorable and dutiful holy warrior St. Expedite, during thy short life on earth, you gave a most beautiful example of your dedication, loyalty and honor as a soldier and leader, you taught everyone that there is no condition in which we cannot prevail. Have pity on me. I am in much need of God's Mercy. Obtain for me through thy merits and intercession, the special favor which I now fervently implore (state your petition)*

*Our Father, Hail Mary, Glory be (say each of these prayers)*

*Pray for me, St. Expedite, that my petition be answered with expediency and is worthy of the promises of Christ.*

### Second day

*Preface: Oh most merciful Lord, I humbly prostrate myself before Thy Infinite Majesty, and dedicate to Thy glory the devout prayers which I now present to Thee, as an act of devotion to your servant, St Expedite, whose intercession I am now implor-*

*ing.*

*Glorious St. Expedite, I admire you how quickly you act on any occasion to fulfill your duty. Have pity on me. I am in much need of God's Mercy. Obtain for me through thy merits and intercession, the special favor which I now fervently implore (state your petition)*

*Our Father, Hail Mary, Glory be (say each of these prayers)*

*Pray for me, St. Expedite, that my petition be answered with expediency and is worthy of the promises of Christ.*

### Third day
*Preface: Oh most merciful Lord, I humbly prostrate myself before Thy Infinite Majesty, and dedicate to Thy glory the devout prayers which I now present to Thee, as an act of devotion to your servant, St Expedite, whose intercession I am now imploring.*

*Glorious St. Expedite, testing and suffering were never avoided. You knew and accepted your fate with courage and confidence. Have pity on me. I am in much need of God's Mercy. Obtain for me through thy merits and intercession, the special favor which I now fervently implore (state your petition)*

*Our Father, Hail Mary, Glory be (say each of these prayers)*

*Pray for me, St. Expedite, that my petition be answered with expediency and is worthy of the promises of Christ.*

# Daily Prayer to St. Expedite

This is a general prayer that can be said as part of a daily devotion to St. Expedite. You can light a white votive or tealight candle to him for your daily devotional. Begin by making the sign of the cross and saying the following while doing so:

*"In the name of the Father and of the Son and of the Holy Spirit. Amen."*

Then, say the following prayer:

*Lord, our God and Father,*
*you allow us to invoke St. Expedite*
*as intercessor, especially in cases that we consider urgent;*
*I pray that you hear my plea.*
*Help me to overcome this difficult time;*
*Protect me from anything that might harm me;*
*Help my family and friends.*
*Give us peace, tranquility and grace.*
*Through Christ our Lord. Amen.*

As always, when he answers your petition, offer him some red flowers or a slice of pound cake with 3 nickels pressed into the cake (nickels optional). Offerings should be made immediately upon learning of his response.

# Minute Prayer to the Minute Saint

This prayer is to be said when you have just a minute to request something you need immediately. Sit before his image and snap your fingers three times then pray:

*Martyr and our protector, St Espidee.*
*You who know the needs that challenge us,*
*I beg you to intercede before the Holy Trinity and grant me the*
*grace of (state your petition)*
*if it is for the good of our souls.*
*Through Christ our Lord.*
*Amen.*

*GLORIOUS ST ESPIDEE*
*Pray for us.*

As always, when he answers your petition, offer him some red flowers or a slice of pound cake, with 3 nickels pressed into the cake (nickels optional). Offerings should be made immediately upon learning of his response.

# General Prayer of Devotion to St. Expedite

Light white candle to St. Expedite for a general devotional. When he answers your petition, make an immediate public statement of gratitude. You may also give him some flowers.

*St. Expedite honored*
*By the gratitude of those*
*who have invoked thee*
*at the last hour*
*and for pressing cases,*
*I pray to thee to obtain*
*from the all powerful*
*Goodness of God,*
*By the intercession*
*Of Mary Immaculate,*
*The grace we solicit with*
*All submission*
*To the Divine Will.*
*Amen*

# Devotional Prayer to St. Expedite

Light white candle to St. Expedite for a general devotional. As always, after he answers your petition, immediately give him public thanks and offer him some flowers.

*O God,*
*Come to my assistance;*
*Lord, make haste to help me.*
*My dear Jesus,*
*Through the powerful intercession*
*of your faithful servant,*
*St. Expedite,*
*may I receive every grace*
*and help in my current need.*
*May I grow in the virtue of*
*patient endurance so that I*
*may courageously wait*
*upon your timing O Lord.*
*I put my entire trust in you*
*my Jesus, for it is*
*only through your name*
*that we may each be saved.*
*Amen.*
~ Pedro de la Cruz

# Prayer to St. Expedite for Urgent Causes

Light red candle to St. Expedite for an urgent request. As always, after he answers your petition, immediately give him public thanks and offer him some red flowers, white rum or a slice of pound cake if you have promised it to him.

*My Saint Expedite of urgent and just causes,*
*please intercede for me with Our Lord Jesus Christ*
*Succor me in this hour of affliction and despair,*
*You who are a Holy warrior,*
*You who are the Saint of the afflicted,*
*You who are the Saint of the desperate,*
*you who are the Saint of urgent causes,*
*Protect me, Help me,*
*Give me Strength, Courage and Serenity.*
*Hear my plea. _____*
*(Clearly express what you want, and ask him to find a way to get it to you.)*
*My Saint Expedite,*
*help me to prevail through these difficult hours,*
*protect me from all those who want to harm me,*
*respond to my plea with urgency.*
*Bring me back to the state of peace and tranquility,*
*my Saint Expedite.*
*I will be grateful to you for the rest of my life*
*and I will speak your name to all those who have faith.*
*Amen.*

# Prayer to St. Expedite for Expediency

Light a red candle to St. Expedite for quick results. Be sure to immediately thank him publicly and fulfill your vow when he grants your petition.

*Saint Expedite,*
*Noble Roman Youth, Martyr,*
*You who quickly brings things to pass,*
*You who never delays,*
*I come to you in need —*

(state your petition)

*Do this for me St. Expedite,*
*And when it is accomplished,*
*I will as rapidly reply for my part*
*With an offering to you.*

(State your vow or promise)

*Be Quick, St. Expedite!*
*Grant my wish before your candle burns out,*
*And I will magnify your name.*
*Amen.*

Remember, whatever your vow is, you must fulfill that vow with expediency. Failure to do so can be interpreted as a slight and he may take back what he gave you.

# Novena to St. Expedite

Similar to the *Nine Hour Novena* described in the previous chapter, this novena is to be said over a period of nine days. In this novena, St. Expedite is petitioned to intercede for us for all the graces that we need in our life, from the gift of hope to the gift of final perseverance. The novena is to be said following this structure each day:

1. Make the sign of the cross.
2. Pray the *Act of Contrition* (see page 115)
3. Say the general prayer to St. Expedite (below).
4. Say the specific prayer for the specific day.
5. Make your petition (your petition should be the same one each day. Do not ask for something different each day).
6. Pray one *Our Father, three Hail Marys* and a *Glory Be*
7. End with making the sign of the cross.

## General Prayer to St. Expedite
## (to be said each day)
*Glorious St. Expedite !*
*Great have been the merits of your unshakable faith in us.*
*Be our guide and help us to walk with hope and courage in our earthly life. We pray fervently for relief to our suffering and seek your Divine intercession to open the gates of heaven to the keys of life that await us. Through Christ our Lord.*
*Amen.*

Invocation: *St. Expedite, courageous defender of righteousness pray for us who have recourse to thee.*

**Day One: Faith**
*O Glorious Martyr, Saint Expedite, through the lively faith which was granted you by Bon Dieu (God), I ask you to awaken the same faith in my heart, that I may also believe wholeheart-*

edly that there is a Good God, but Most importantly that I may be saved from offending Him.

*St. Expedite, courageous defender of righteousness, pray for us who have recourse to thee.*

### Day Two: Hope
*St. Expedite, I turn to you with the hope that you can help me in this most urgent situation. I pray that my heart radiates optimism, so I can recognize the moments each day that are unique and signs of all that is Divine. Give me the ability to discover new alternatives, where today I only see confusion, doubt and fatigue. Hear my plea and hear my request, because I need you now more than ever.*

**Make your petition.**

*St. Expedite, courageous defender of righteousness, pray for us who have recourse to thee.*

### Day Three: Availability
*St. Expedite, you who are always available to assist in just and urgent causes, hear my prayers and bring me your help today. Show me which path I should follow, guide each of my steps and open the way free from storms. I trust you alone can help me. Come to my aid and show me a ray of sunlight that will illuminate my soul.*

**Make your petition.**

*St. Expedite, courageous defender of righteousness, pray for us who have recourse to thee.*

### Day Four: Justice
*St. Expedite, you have a righteous heart, bring justice to the daily injustices that surround me, show me that it is possible to*

change the situations that disturb me today. Guide each of my words to be clear in adversity, because I know if my mind is clear it will be easier to make the right decision in such confusion.

**Make your petition.**

*St. Expedite, courageous defender of justice, pray for us who have recourse to thee.*

### Day Five: Humility
*St. Expedite, teach me to have a humble heart like yours because I need to learn the value of humility. Transform my pride into humility expressed in my daily acts. I trust that you will teach me how.*

**Make your petition.**

*St. Expedite, courageous defender of righteousness, pray for us who have recourse to thee.*

### Day Six: Detachment
*O Glorious St. Expedite, through the bountiful graces you received from Heaven, grant that I may get rid of all the feelings, self-defeating thoughts and behaviors that block my way to self actualization.*

**Make your petition.**

*St. Expedite, courageous defender of righteousness, pray for us who have recourse to thee.*

### Day Seven: Charity
*St. Expedite, plant my seed of love to share with others the joy of finding you. That charity is for me a gift of Divine Providence to sow faith in other hearts. I am confident that you will*

*help me in adversity and will guide my steps so you can exercise charity among my brothers and sisters.*

**Make your petition.**

*St. Expedite, courageous defender of righteousness, pray for us who have recourse to thee.*

### Day Eight: Courage
*St. Expedite, fill my heart with courage to face my fears today. Guide my steps as a brave soldier of justice. Make me strong in soul and spirit to keep going in these days when fear dominates my life. You who were a brave man, teach me to live with my fears and my daily pains, so that I can succeed and triumph in spite of adversity.*

**Make your petition.**

*St. Expedite, courageous defender of righteous, pray for us who have recourse to thee.*

### Day Nine:  Final Perseverance
*O Glorious Martyr, Saint Expedite, who was so much loved by the Queen of Heaven, that to you nothing was denied, ask her, please my advocate, that through the sufferings of her Divine Son and her own sorrows, I may receive this day the grace I ask of you; but above all the grace to die first before I commit any mortal sin. Amen.*

**Make your petition.**

*St. Expedite, courageous defender of righteousness, pray for us who have recourse to thee.*

# Litany of St. Expedite

A litany is a well-known and much appreciated form of responsive petition, used in public liturgical services, and in private devotions, for common necessities of the Church, or in calamities—to implore God's aid or to appease His just wrath (Mershman, 1910).

*Oh St. Expedite, who didst receive from the Lord the crown of righteousness which He has promised to those who love Him, pray for me.*
*St. Expedite, invincible warrior of the Faith, pray for me.*
*St. Expedite, faithful unto death, pray for me.*
*St. Expedite, patron of youth, pray for me.*
*San expeditious, help of scholars, pray for me.*
*St. Expedite, protector of travelers, pray for me.*
*St. Expedite, advocate of sinners, pray for me.*
*St. Expedite, salvation of the sick, pray for me.*
*St. Expedite, model soldier, pray for me.*
*St. Expedite, mediator of lawsuits, pray for me.*
*St. Expedite, helper in urgent matters, pray for me.*
*St. Expedite, slayer of procrastination, pray for me.*
*St. Expedite, faithful supporter of those who have hope in you, pray for me.*
*St. Expedite, I beg, do not leave for tomorrow what you can do today, come to my assistance.*

*Jesus, Lamb of God who takes away the sin of the world, forgive me Lord.*
*Jesus, Lamb of God who takes away the sin of the world, hear me Lord.*
*Jesus, Lamb of God who takes away the sin of the world, have mercy of my Lord.*
*Jesus, hear me.*
*Jesus, hear my prayer.*
*My voice comes to you, Lord.*

*Let us pray:*
*Almighty and Eternal God, Who art the consolation of the af-*
*flicted and the support of those in pain, deign to receive the*
*cries of our distress, so that by the intercession and merits of*
*thy glorious martyr, St Expeditus, we may joyfully experience*
*in our extreme necessity the help of thy mercy, through Christ*
*Our Lord.*

*AMEN.*

Light a white candle and burn some frankincense incense.
Repeat the above litany one time and then offer one Our Father, Hail Mary and Glory Be in thanksgiving—and a public
statement of thanks, of course— for any favors received. Offering him red flowers is also a nice gesture.

# Standard Catholic Prayers used in the Novenas to St. Expedite

## The Our Father

The Our Father is the oldest of Christian prayers, going back to Jesus Christ himself, who, in Matthew 6:9-13, taught his disciples to pray in these words. Because the prayer is believed to have come from Christ, it is used in every Mass.

*Our Father who art in heaven, hallowed be Thy name; Thy Kingdom come; Thy will be done on earth as it is in heaven. Give us this day our daily bread; and forgive us our trespasses, as we forgive those who trespass against us; and lead us not into temptation, but deliver us from evil. Amen.*

## Memorare to the Blessed Virgin Mary

The Memorare of the Blessed Virgin Mary is one of the best known of all Marian prayers. It is a section of a much longer 15th-century prayer known as the "Ad sanctitatis tuae pedes, dulcissima Virgo Maria." By the early 16th century, Catholics had begun to treat the Memorare as a separate prayer, and Fr. Claude Bernard, a French priest who ministered to the imprisoned and those condemned to death, was a zealous advocate of the prayer. He attributed the conversion of many criminals to the intercession of the Blessed Virgin Mary, invoked through the Memorare.

*Remember, O Most gracious Virgin Mary, that never was it known that any one who fled to thy protection, implored thy help, or sought thy intercession was left unaided. Inspired with this confidence, I fly unto thee, O Virgin of virgins, my Mother. To thee do I come, before thee I stand, sinful and sorrowful. O Mother of the Word Incarnate, despise not my petitions, but in thy mercy hear and answer me. Amen.*

# The Hail Mary

The Hail Mary is a traditional Catholic prayer asking for the intercession of the Virgin Mary, the mother of Jesus.

*Hail Mary, full of grace! the Lord is with thee; blessed art thou among women, and blessed is the fruit of thy womb, Jesus. Holy Mary, Mother of God, pray for us sinners, now and at the hour of our death. Amen.*

# Final Thoughts

There are quite a few folks who come to me and say they have performed the novena or done another such ritual to St. Expedite and he didn't come through for them. I have attempted to include as many details and ways to go about invoking his intercession, that if you have done everything according to the letter and he still hasn't come through, then my advice is to rethink what you are asking of him.

For example, are you asking to win the multimillion dollar lottery? While this is a request many people will to turn supernatural means for attaining, it is highly unlikely he will grant such a wish. Now, I cannot say he has never done so, but I can say I have never heard of him doing so. If you have asked and he hasn't responded, then perhaps it would be better to ask for something more realistic, like for a specific amount of money to pay a specific bill by a specific date. There are no limitations on how many times you can petition him so, start with a reasonable request and he will be much more likely to help you.

Also, pay attention to the words you speak when invoking his intercession. Although I pointed it out in the book already, it is worthwhile pointing out again the caveat in one of the popular Catholic prayers to him, *"if it is for the good of our souls."* If you are petitioning him with that built in caveat, then you are giving him an out. If you are asking for something that is not ultimately good for you, and you have told him in your supplication not to grant it if it is not good for your soul, then guess what? He won't do it. So, tweak your prayers, or be okay with the standard ones, because praying from the heart is part and parcel for working with St. Expedite. If you don't mean what you say, then why should he listen?

Another issue that I observe that tends to impede success,

or stop success dead in its tracks, is the lack of urgency some folks feel to pay him after he responds. They will say, "Oh I need to go tomorrow to get him his pound cake," for example. Well, why would you wait to pay him when you ask him to act with the utmost expediency on his part? Be prepared with the offerings you have promised him. Have that pound cake in the freezer—that's one reason why Sarah Lee pound cake is so ideal. It can be frozen and retrieved in an instant. Have that bottle of white rum in the cabinet. Be willing to run to the store and buy him some flowers—and make them red roses if you promised him red roses. Remember roses are expensive, so don't promise a dozen if you can't afford it. In fact, if you don't have a florist or grocery store that regularly carries the kind of flowers you promise him, then it is probably better to just say you will give him some flowers. Then, whatever they have in stock will work and you won't find yourself in the position of being unable to fulfill your vow.

Be realistic with your supplications. He may be a miracle saint, but he won't make world peace. That would entail putting him in the position of the Ultimate Creator and stripping people of their free will. I am pretty sure there is not a conjurer on this planet with that kind of power. Be specific with what you need, give him a deadline if you are up against one. In other words, be thoughtful, be intentional and be deliberate with the words you speak, and you are much more likely to see results with St. Expedite.

I wish you much luck with your spiritual and conjuring endeavors with St. Expedite. Treat him with respect, develop a relationship with him and he will be loyal and devoted to you. That is something I can tell you I know from personal experience and have heard from countless devotees. The intensity of your devotion will be matched and surpassed by the intensity of his love for you. He is a servant of Bon Dieu and as such, it is his duty to intercede on our behalf. And as a soldier, he does so with the utmost commitment and urgency. Glory be to St. Espidee!

# References

Anonymous, (1920). *The New Royal Cookbook*. Royal Baking Powder Co.

Besançon, A. and Jane Marie Todd. (2000). *The Forbidden Image: An Intellectual History of Iconoclasm*. Chicago: University of Chicago Press.

Black, C. (2011). *Profile of Cinnamon Black*. You tube video.

Carpio, G. (2008). *Laughing Fit to Kill: Black Humor in the Fictions of Slavery*. New York: Oxford University Press.

Harvey, K. (2008). Wild Island Reunion. *Expressions Magazine*.

Hémard, N. (2013). *New Orleans Nostalgia: Prohibition in New Orleans*. Retrieved from: http://www.neworleansbar.org/new-orleans-nostalgia.html

Hyatt, H. M. (1973). *Hoodoo-Conjuration-Witchcraft-Rootwork*. Hannibal, MO: Western Publishing, Inc.

Iconoclasm. (2014, April 2). *New World Encyclopedia*, . Retrieved 06:09, December 13, 2014 from http://www.newworldencyclopedia.org/p/index.php?title=Iconoclasm&oldid=979939.

Malbrough, R. (2003). *Hoodoo Mysteries*. St Paul, Minnesota: Llewellyn Publications.

Mershman, F. (1910). Litany. In *The Catholic Encyclopedia*. New York: Robert Appleton Company. Retrieved December 2, 2014 from New Advent: http://www.newadvent.org/cathen/09286a.htm

Métraux, A. (1974). *Voodoo,* London: Sphere Books Limited.

Musée de France, (n.d.). *Catacombs.* Retrieved from: http://www.catacombes.paris.fr/en/catacombs

19th April. *Expeditus, commander of the Thunder and martyr legion.* Retrieved from: http://hodiemecum.hautetfort.com /archive/2008/04/19/19-avril-saint-expedit-commandant -de-la-legion-fulminante-et.html.

nolaskullandbones.blogspot.com

O'Brien , M. S. (2004). *Saint Expedtitus Don't Get No Respect.* Retrieved from the website Aliens in this World: suburbanbanshee.wordpress.com/2004/04/17/

Picardo, N. (2007). Semantic Homicide' and the So-called Reserve Heads: The Theme of Decapitation in Egyptian Funerary Religion and Some Implications for the Old Kingdom. *Journal of the American Research Center in Egypt, 23.*

Ravenscroft, T. (1987). *Spear of Destiny.* York Beach, ME: Samuel Weiser, Inc.

White, William. (2013). pp. 106-7. *Notes and Queries* (Vol. 5). London: Forgotten Books. (Original work published 1908)

Williams, K. (2011). St Expedito's Role in South Louisiana Catholicism, in New Orleans and in the Italian-American Community near Independence, Louisiana, *Louisiana Folklore Miscellany*, Volume 65.

# Creole Moon Publications Ordering Information

# Conjuring Black Hawk

## Discover the Secrets of a Hidden New Orleans Conjure Tradition

### Denise Alvarado

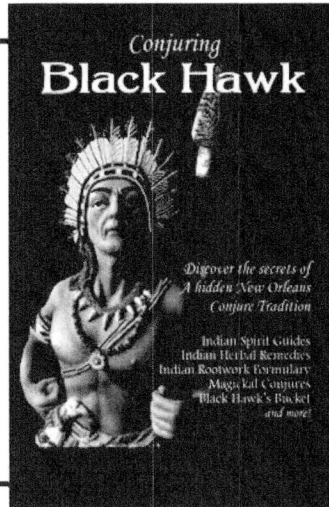

Never before has a book been written about Father Black Hawk from the perspective of a Creole Native who has walked inside the longhouses, sat in the sweat lodges, cried on a hill for a vision, and received the mysteries through these traditional, intertribal Native American ceremonies. The information contained in these pages will blow your mind, burst apart the stereotypes, and give Father Black Hawk the final say in how he should be honored and served. The reader should set aside all expectations for what they think they know, and be ready for a true and authentic cultural smorgasbord of Southern Conjure Indian medicine.

It has been long identified that Father Black Hawk found his way to New Orleans by Spiritualist Mother Leafy Anderson. Indian Spirit Guides are not uncommon in the Spritualist Churches; however, Father Black Hawk is indeed unique in his presence in the New Orleans area. Not only is he revered in the Spiritualist Churches, he is also recognized and honored within the New Orleans Voudou pantheon of spirits. He has also found his way onto the altars of Hoodoo and conjure practitioners nationwide. But, there has been a strong Native American presence in Louisiana long before Black Hawk arrived, making his manifestation and assimilation into the various Creole spiritual traditions both easy and logical.

To order, visit
http://conjuringblackhawk.weebly.com/

# Our Titles

| Title | Price |
|---|---|
| Conjuring Black Hawk: Discover the Secrets of a Hidden New Orleans Conjure Tradition<br>By Denise Alvarado | $24.95 |
| The Conjurer's Guide to St. Expedite<br>By Denise Alvarado | $14.95 |
| Crossroads Mamas 105 Spiritual Baths For Every Occasion<br>By Denise Alvarado and Madrina Angelique | $9.95 |
| Workin' in da Boneyard<br>By Denise Alvarado and Madrina Angelique | $9.95 |
| Day of the Dead Handbook<br>By Denise Alvarado | $13.00 |
| Hoodoo Almanac 2012<br>By Denise Alvarado, Carolina Dean and Alyne Pustanio | $19.95 |
| Hoodoo Almanac 2013 Gazette<br>By Denise Alvarado, Carolina Dean and Alyne Pustanio | $19.95 |
| Hoodoo Almanac 2014 and 2015 (Two full years in one volume)<br>By Denise Alvarado, Carolina Dean and Alyne Pustanio | $19.95 |
| Voodoo Dolls in Magick and Ritual<br>By Denise Alvarado | $15.95 |
| The True Grimoire<br>By King Solomon | $6.95 |
| Conjure Diary<br>By Denise Alvarado | $12.95 |
| Gypsy Wisdom, Spells Charms and Folklore<br>By Denise Alvarado | $13.00 |
| Fortune Telling with Playing Cards<br>By P.R.S. Foli | $6.95 |
| Hoodoo and Conjure Quarterly Premiere Issue<br>By Multiple authors, Denise Alvarado, Editor/Contributor | $44.95 |
| Hoodoo and Conjure Quarterly #2<br>By Multiple authors, Denise Alvarado, Editor/Contributor | $17.95 |
| Hoodoo and Conjure New Orleans<br>By Multiple authors, Denise Alvarado, Editor/Contributor | $24.95 |
| Hoodoo and Conjure New Orleans 2014<br>By Multiple authors, Denise Alvarado, Editor/Contributor | $24.95 |
| Purloined Stories and Early Tales of Old New Orleans<br>By Alyne Pustanio | $15.95 |

# Creole Moon Publications Order Form

| Item # | Description | Qty. | Price | Subtotal |
|--------|-------------|------|-------|----------|
|        |             |      |       |          |
|        |             |      |       |          |
|        |             |      |       |          |
|        |             |      |       |          |
|        |             |      |       |          |
|        |             |      |       |          |
|        |             |      |       |          |
|        |             |      |       |          |

Order Total _____

Tax _____

Shipping _____

Total _____

Name

Address

Phone

Shipping is $5.15 for the first title and $2.00 for each additional title. Domestic shipping through mail order only. International shipping is $8.15 per title.

Please make your check or money order out to Denise Alvarado.

Send check or money order to:

Denise Alvarado
P.O. Box 25687
Prescott Valley, AZ 86312

Printed by Amazon Italia Logistica S.r.l.
Torrazza Piemonte (TO), Italy

53098714R00087